Reshaping
TEACHING IN
HIGHER
EDUCATION

Staff and Educational Development Series
Series Editor: James Wisdom

SEDA is the Staff and Educational Development Association. It supports and encourages developments in teaching and learning in higher education through a variety of methods: publications, conferences, networking, journals, regional meetings and research – and through various SEDA Accreditation Schemes.

SEDA
Selly Wick House
59–61 Selly Wick Road
Selly Park
Birmingham B29 7JE
Tel: 0121–415 6801
Fax: 0121–415 6802
E-mail: office@seda.demon.co.uk

Reshaping
TEACHING IN HIGHER EDUCATION

Linking Teaching with Research

Alan Jenkins, Rosanna Breen & Roger Lindsay
with Angela Brew

SEDA
STAFF AND EDUCATIONAL
DEVELOPMENT ASSOCIATION

KOGAN
PAGE

London and Sterling, VA

First published in Great Britain and the United States in 2003 by Kogan Page
Limited

Kogan Page Limited   22883 Quicksilver Drive
120 Pentonville Road   Sterling VA 20166–2012
London N1 9JN   USA
UK
www.kogan-page.co.uk

ISBN 0 7494 3903 3 (pbk)
ISBN 0 7494 3902 5 (hbk)

British Library Cataloguing in Publication Data

A CIP record for this book is available from the British Library.

Library of Congress Cataloging in Publication Data

Reshaping teaching in higher education : linking teaching with research/
Alan Jenkins ... [et al.].
    p. cm. – (Staff and education and development series)
Includes bibliographical references (p.) and index.
  ISBN 0-7494-3902-5
  1. Education, Higher – Research. 2. College teaching. I. Jenkins,
Alan, 1940- II. Series.
  LB2326.3 .R49 2003
  378. 1′2–dc21
                    2002014808

Typeset by Saxon Graphics Ltd, Derby
Printed and bound in Great Britain by Creative Print and Design (Wales), Ebbw Vale

Contents

Notes on the authors

Rosanna Breen, a research psychologist, is currently a Senior Researcher in the Faculty of Education, University of Cambridge, researching aspects of postgraduate studies. Previously she was a researcher in the Oxford Centre for Staff and Learning Development at Oxford Brookes University. She specializes in discipline specific student motivation to learn, and for her doctorate she developed a model of motivation, capable of predicting student learning behaviour and performance. She spent four years designing and implementing other research programmes for Oxford Brookes, which employed a variety of quantitative and qualitative methodologies. These included an evaluation of IT based learning methods and studies of undergraduate and postgraduate attitudes towards lecturer research and how student motivation is shaped by (staff) research.

Dr Angela Brew is Senior Lecturer in the Institute for Teaching and Learning at the University of Sydney. She has worked in the area of academic development for over 20 years and has researched in the area of teaching and learning in higher education and related fields in the UK and in Australia. Her particular interests are in research as a process of learning. More broadly, she is interested in the process of how we come to know and in what that knowing consists. For her thesis she developed guidelines for post-positivist research. Her latest book (Brew, 2001a), *The Nature of Research: Inquiry in academic contexts,* was published by Routledge Falmer in August 2001. She is President of the Higher Education Research and Development Society of Australasia (HERDSA).

Professor Alan Jenkins is an educational developer/researcher in the Westminster Institute, Oxford Brookes University. In previous academic incarnations he taught and researched geography, and was then a member of the Oxford Centre for Staff Development and Learning at Brookes, for whom he now acts as a tutor on the ILT accredited course for new academic staff. His particular interests lie in linking staff in the disciplines with the generic research and scholarship on higher education, and also in linking the worlds of generic educational developers with the particular worlds of the disciplines. At Brookes he has university wide roles on linking teaching and research and developing pedagogic research. He is project adviser to the national Fund for the Development of Teaching and Learning: Project LINK, on linking teaching and research in Built Environment Disciplines (http://www.brookes.ac.uk/schools/planning/LTRC/) and Project Director for a Learning and Teaching Support Network project on Linking Teaching and Research in the Disciplines (http://www.brookes.ac.uk/genericlink/).

Roger Lindsay is a Principal Lecturer in the Department of Psychology at Oxford Brookes University. Roger began his academic career as a philosopher, but made a full recovery, completing a DPhil in Psychology at the University of Oxford as part of his rehabilitation programme. He is interested in a wide range of problems in psychology and cognition. Roger sees pedagogic research as the area where his professional interests as a teacher and his academic interests as a researcher come together. Roger has been involved in many pedagogic research projects over the years, including studies of the effects of class size, workload and paid employment on student achievement in HE. He has worked with Alan Jenkins on student perceptions of lecturer research activity, and with Rosanna Breen on discipline specific knowledge and student motivation. His current preoccupations centre on what leads students to learn the particular things they do, and what memory systems and processes subserve the learning that takes place.

Preface

Angela Brew

The drive to bring teaching and research closer together is perhaps one of the most significant developments in thinking about teaching and learning in higher education in recent years. Manifestations of new thinking about this relationship can be seen in many countries. These have been given impetus by a confluence of developments in research which has questioned the veracity of the relationship; funding policies of national governments which have threatened to drive a wedge between teaching and research institutions and activities; and concerns throughout the academic community about the nature of mass higher education and the knowledge and skills needing to be developed in students to prepare them for an uncertain and complex world.

This volume, building on the research literature, critically examines policy and looks positively at how, within a sometimes difficult and alien context, individual academics, course teams, departments, institutions as a whole and government and professional bodies can turn their attention to actively fostering the links between teaching and research. This is hitherto uncharted territory, and in this pioneering work the authors have drawn on an impressive range of examples from Australia, Canada, New Zealand, the UK, the United States and Hong Kong to provide guidance.

But why should we try to bring teaching and research more closely together? What are the motivations for doing so? Is this just a bid on the part of research intensive universities to prop up the research enterprise, or a cry of help from less research focused institutions to ensure that a wedge is not drawn between research institutions and teaching institutions? While these may be at the forefront of the minds of some academic managers and policy makers, what motivates this volume is the conviction that what drives the movement to bring teaching and research closer together is improvements in the quality of the student learning experience. Involving students in inquiry – in research – is a way of improving their learning, motivating them more. After all, what motivates large numbers of academics is engaging in the excitement of research. Bringing research and teaching together is a way of enhancing the motivation of both academics and students.

But that is not all. In a world characterized by uncertainty and what Ron Barnett (2000) calls 'supercomplexity' we need, not bodies of pre-defined knowledge, but rather the skills of finding out. Knowledge has become fluid and contestable. In its many domains of discourse it has become a product of communication and negotiation. The students of the future are going to need the skills of inquiry – of research – if they are to be able to investigate and to learn and hence be employable in the future. In such a world the authority of the 'teacher' is continually questioned. So students need to understand how knowledge is constructed. Since it is through research that new knowledge is created, students are going to have to become researchers to survive and thrive in the complex, pluralistic world of the future.

So strategies for bringing research and teaching together, such as are contained in this volume, are strategies for enhancing the capacity of academic communities and the wider social world, to engage in lifelong learning through the continual process of systematic collection and examination of evidence, and critical reflection on that evidence as a basis for learning and action. Viewed in this light, this volume goes beyond narrow conceptions of research as discovery, to place inquiry centre stage in higher education practice.

We are already familiar with case based, scenario based and problem based curricula where students' learning is organized around carefully structured inquiry processes. But we are also familiar with the difficulty that many academic teachers face when they try to implement such approaches alongside traditional lecture based teaching or in institutional contexts that are unsympathetic to challenges to the *status quo*, or where support structures for teaching and learning make changes to timetables or class organization difficult. The move to bring teaching and research closer together provides a rationale and a context for the transformation of structures which inhibit the development of new approaches to teaching and learning. This volume contains a cornucopia of examples of ways in which institutions and their academic units can free up the possibilities for a productive relationship between the research that academics do and the learning of their students.

Central to the movement to bring research and teaching together is an enhanced notion of what we understand research to be. Also central is the development of our understanding of how research and teaching might be brought together in particular contexts, disciplinary and departmental, and what the implications are for our particular institutions. We are on a journey and we do not know what the destination looks like. Initiatives to bring teaching and research together have the potential to change our ideas about what a higher education should be, and they also have the potential to alter radically relationships between academics and students. But even if we have more modest aims there is something in this volume to guide and sustain the steps we take. In our institutions, in our departments and in our work groups, we need individually and collectively to reflect on what the 'nexus' so called, means for us.

In this volume we have a map to help us on our way. Developments across the world highlighted here provide beacons to guide us. Precedents have been set. Paths have been laid. Fare thee well!

Angela Brew, University of Sydney, Australia

Acknowledgements

This publication grew out of research initiated by Tim Blackman (now Director of Social Sciences and Law at the University of Teesside, UK) soon after he was appointed Deputy Head of Social Sciences at Oxford Brookes (UK), with a responsibility for developing research. The context was the institutional commitment to improving the school's research base. Inside the institution and within the school some feared that this increased focus on research would be at the expense of the institution's long commitment to, and reputation for, quality teaching. These concerns prompted Blackman to initiate research studies in which Alan Jenkins, Rosanna Breen and Roger Lindsay from Oxford Brookes (with Renee Paton-Saltzberg) became centrally involved. It also led to university-wide discussions and actions to ensure that undergraduate and postgraduate students benefited from the increased institutional commitment to staff research.

Those research studies and policy actions on teaching and research relations, which are still ongoing, have put us in contact with many academics with kindred concerns in the UK and internationally. In the UK we have gained much from a group that was initiated and led by Roger Brown, Principal of Southampton Institute. This group of researchers and educational developers has periodically met to share ideas and attempt to shape national policies. But these issues are not just UK based; they are of international concern, even though their form may vary in the way research and teaching in higher education are conceived, funded and organized. Academics worldwide, particularly from North America and Australasia, have considerably aided our thinking and contributed through their publications, e-mails and discussions at conferences and research visits. This book draws on and celebrates their work, and hopefully contributes to the thinking and actions of academics and institutions worldwide, with very different institutional missions and contrasting priorities between research and teaching.

Finally we gratefully acknowledge the support of SEDA (Small Grants Scheme) in financially contributing to this publication, to Neil Thew and Linda France (University of Sussex) and James Wisdom and Jonathan Simpson (Kogan Page) for their editorial suggestions and support, and to Susan Curran (Curran Publishing Services) for detailed supportive copy-editing.

1

Overview: reshaping teaching in higher education to support the links between teaching and research

The University's account argues strongly for the continuing and crucial value of the link between teaching and research... In practice ... the audit team found that there was very little systematic reflection within the University about just what was meant by the claimed inter-dependence of research and teaching.
(Higher Education Quality Council, 1997: 3 Audit of Exeter University)

The research universities have too often failed, and continue to fail, their undergraduate populations: ... thousands of students graduate without ever seeing the world-famous professors or tasting genuine research.
(Boyer Commission, University of Stony Brook, 1998: 3)

I believe that the main hope for realising a genuinely student centred undergraduate education lies in re-engineering the teaching–research nexus.
(Ramsden, 2001: 4)

Our aim in this book is to help individual staff, course teams, departments, institutions and national systems to make effective linkages between discipline based research and student learning: in effect to 'reshape teaching' and much more of universities and academic organizations, to ensure more effective linkages between student learning and research.

The relationship between (staff) research and student learning is a long-standing and controversial issue, and in the next chapter we review that research evidence. In brief, while many, perhaps most, academics and institutional mission statements see good teaching as being intimately related to quality research, that tight coupling is not supported by much of the research evidence. Much of that evidence would question that 'nexus'. Indeed some researchers and commentators would see staff research, and staff commitment to research, as an irrelevance or even an obstacle to improving teaching quality. Some would agree with a remark attributed to the economist Milton Friedman, 'There are many activities that have little to do with higher education: namely, athletics and research.'

Organizations such as the Staff and Educational Development Association (SEDA) and their equivalents in other countries, and the staff involved in such organizations, have generally focused their energies on issues to do with teaching methods, assessment and so on, and on the professionalization of teaching and teachers in higher education. The research that is explicitly valued by such organizations and individuals is that which is generic to teaching and learning in higher education, and to a lesser extent about the teaching of the disciplines.

Staff research in the disciplines *per se*, from art history to zoology, has largely been either ignored or even questioned by such organizations and individuals, particularly in the context of its possible distortion of individual and institutional priorities to research at the neglect of teaching, and the perceived priority to research performance in decisions over promotion. One of us (Jenkins) does consider that research in the disciplines has been given far too much priority in decisions over promotion and institutional prestige and thus has effectively devalued (individual) staff and institutional commitment to teaching.

But even if that view of misplaced priority given to discipline based research in decisions over promotion and institutional recognition etc is accepted, it still leaves open whether (staff) discipline based research is valuable to student learning, and if so how it can be 'organized' better to ensure that students learn effectively in a context where some or all staff are involved in discipline based research.

In seeking to connect teaching and research, we have placed our focus solely on connecting student learning to the research done on discipline based inquiry. Thus, in the case of students studying art history, the aim of this book is to draw closer connections between their learning of art history and research in art history *per se*.

There are two other important ways of linking teaching and research that are not considered here. The first concerns those staff in art history and so on doing discipline based pedagogic research on aspects of the teaching of art history or on generic issues of teaching. Such research is likely to be published in discipline based pedagogic journals such as *Teaching Sociology* and others (Yorke, 2000). Second are staff in the disciplines reading and using the generic and relevant discipline based research and scholarship on learning and teaching, to improve their courses. This might be called 'evidence-based teaching, or the scholarship of teaching' (Hutchings and Shulman, 1999; Healey, 1999).

Our focus then is on the long-standing issue of whether and how to connect staff research in their discipline, and their knowledge and interest in that research, with student learning. Our perspective is that:

- The (potential) value of staff discipline based research to student learning has to be set in the context of the considerable research evidence that questions that close relationship, certainly at undergraduate level.

- More recent research does demonstrate the (potential) value of staff research to student learning, and for motivating students to learn in higher education. This research also shows that this linkage is not automatic, and indeed has to be carefully built into the curriculum, department, institutional and national planning.

- Questioning the value or possibility of the link also stems from the realities of mass higher education; thus the linkage might once have been readily assumed or delivered with small classes, selective student entry, and staff with time to teach and research effectively. Clearly if that 'golden age' existed, it has now gone.

- While there should be diversity in the foci and priorities of course teams and institutions, we do see an understanding and valuing of research, and to an extent skills at doing research, as being central to what all students should experience in higher education. To us such a linkage is still desirable in the context of mass higher education. Arguably many aspects of society including the needs of the 'knowledge economy' make the linkage more vital than it might have been in that (mythical) 'golden age'.

- We also see involvement in research as central to the motivations of many staff and that potentially this involvement can significantly benefit students.

- While much of what we present here is relevant to both undergraduate and taught postgraduate levels, our central focus is on undergraduate courses, for that is where the research clearly tells us the connections are not automatic or easily made.

- The phrase 'reshaping teaching' in the title brings out a central theme: that this focus will involve reshaping teaching from the level of the individual course or teacher to the whole institution and indeed national systems. But such reshaping starts from much good practice and is strongly based on academic values.

- Paul Ramsden, Pro Vice Chancellor (Learning and Teaching) at the University of Sydney, expressed this book's perspective when he stated, 'the main hope for realising a genuinely student centred undergraduate education lies in re-engineering the research-teaching nexus' (Ramsden, 2001: 4). The word 'engineer' suggests that the link does not occur automatically; it has to be 'designed', 'created', 'constructed', 'contrived', 'brought about'. The word 're-engineer' suggests that even if once the linkage did exist, it now needs significant effort to ensure it is in place, or perhaps better, in many places and processes. Although the focus of the title and the book is about re-shaping teaching in higher education; the effective argument is that if we are really serious about linking teaching and research then actions are needed across much of the academic enterprise, including how research is conceived, organized and funded.

This perspective has determined the organization of this book. In the next two chapters we review the research and scholarly evidence on the linkage, if any, between staff research and quality teaching, and then discuss how to connect student learning, student and staff motivation, and staff research. We then turn to strategies that enable a close 'nexus' between discipline research and student learning to be achieved, and argue that this has to involve action at a variety of levels. In chapter 4 our primary focus is at the level of the individual academic and course team as to how to design and deliver the curriculum. In chapters 5–7 the scale of analysis moves up, to focus first at the level of the institution and then at department, national and international levels.

An overriding theme of the book is that though we see positive benefits to student learning from staff research, that linkage has to be purposefully created at a whole range of levels and by a range of 'actors'. The organization of the book echoes the American scholar Burton Clark's view (1993a) that connections need to be created at three levels: the national system, where he sees the connections are *enabling*; the institutional level, which he sees as *formative;* and the basic unit level (the academic department), which Clark sees as the key *enacting* unit. While our analysis is similar in its emphasis on scales of analysis, we consider that there is also much that individuals and course teams can do, while there is perhaps an increasing role for international disciplinary communities to shape the links. Of that, more later.

We also need to draw attention to the provisional nature of some of the suggestions and ideas presented here. Inside institutions and national systems, academics and policy makers have spent long hours arguing about the existence (or lack of) and value of this linkage. We have spent limited hours on creating and ensuring the linkage exists. For example few of the books on curriculum design consider this issue. In all fairness to Exeter University, the observation that 'there was very little systematic reflection within the University about just what was meant by the claimed interdependence of research and teaching' (HEQC, 1997: 3), is one that could be applied to many institutions, including until recently our own. So we hope this publication will soon be superseded and added to by others to give further substance to the suggestions here.

2

What research and scholarship tell us about teaching–research relationships in higher education

> The strongest policy claim that derives from this Meta analysis is that universities need to set as a mission goal the improvement of the nexus between research and teaching. The goal should not be publish or perish, or teach or impeach, but we beseech you to publish and teach effectively. *The aim is to increase the circumstances in which teaching and research have occasion to meet, and to provide rewards not only for better teaching or for better research but also for demonstrations of the integration between teaching and research.*
> (Hattie and Marsh, 1996: 533; emphasis added)

This book is designed to enhance the linkages between teaching and research. Enhancing that linkage (whether our focus is on the individual academic designing a course or at the level of the whole institution) must recognize that the considerable research evidence challenges the view that there is a natural positive relationship between staff research and student learning. In this chapter we briefly review that evidence, to draw out implications for those of us who wish to increase the positive linkages. The chapter is organized as follows:

- We start by presenting statements of belief and institutional purpose that assert the existence of close positive interconnections between teaching and research.

- In analysing this issue we point to the importance of defining how we model the relationships, and how we conceive both teaching and research. The level of analysis is considered (eg do we study the linkage at the level of the individual academic or say at the level of the course team), as is how institutions and national systems are funded and managed.

- In reviewing the research on this issue, we show that this commonly assumed positive relationship and interdependence is not supported by most of the considerable statistical research evidence, with its central focus at the level of the individual academic.

- However, more recent research has demonstrated that such positive linkages can (and should) occur, but they have to be created or engineered purposefully by individuals, subject groups, institutions and national and international systems.

The potential linkages between (staff) research in the disciplines and student learning are further demonstrated in chapter 3 where we review the research evidence on student and staff motivation. Then, with strong research evidence, we turn to strategies for departmental and institutional course design and national and international management of teaching and research that promise effective linkages between teaching and research.

CLASSIC CONNECTION(S): STATEMENTS OF BELIEF AND VALUE

The close interconnection and interdependence between teaching and research is enshrined in many institutional mission statements (see chapter 5), and more fundamentally in the values and beliefs of many academics worldwide. In the UK, the Robbins Report of 1963 (NCIHE, 1963, para 555) on the then future of higher education saw:

The element of partnership between teacher and taught in a common pursuit of knowledge and understanding, present to some extent in all education, should become the dominant element as the pupil matures and as the intellectual level of work done rises. In the graduate school there are no ultimate authorities, no orthodoxies to which the pupil must subscribe, as he [sic] finds himself taking his part, however humbly and modestly, in the task of making experience intelligible, and illuminating areas of ignorance. It is true that only a minority of undergraduates have the ability and the wish to pursue their studies at a postgraduate level, but the presence of work at this level gives intellectual and spiritual vitality to work at all levels in institutions where it is pursued. It is of the utmost importance that the ablest, who are capable of going forward to original work, should be infected at their first entry to higher education with a sense of the potentialities of their studies.

Though this is a British source, it represents views that have been powerful and at times dominant in recent western thinking on the roles of universities. Thus the American scholar Burton Clark argues:

> research activity can and does serve as an important mode of teaching and a valuable means of learning... student involvement in research is an efficacious way to educate throughout the education system the great mass of students, as well as the elite performers, for the inquiring society into which we are rapidly moving.
> (Clark, 1997: 242)

To take but one more example, Ron Cooke, then Vice Chancellor of York University and, here more significantly, Chair of the UK Higher Education Funding Council's Learning and Teaching Committee stated that:

> One of the enduring memories I have taken with me from when I had a real job as a desert geomorphologist is that all the issues of teaching and learning ultimately focus more on individuals and disciplines than on institutions and government policies; and quality of teaching performance is more a function of intellectual substance, and of individual intelligence, vision, enthusiasm and knowledge, than it is teaching competencies, although of course all are important. These memories underlie my continuing prejudice *that the best teaching and learning is led by the best researchers, provided that they are appropriately trained to teach, a view that may well explain why there is such a high correlation in the UK between Teaching Quality Audit (TQA) and Research Assessment Scores.*
> (Cooke, 1998: 283; emphasis added)

MODELS, DEFINITIONS AND RESEARCH METHODOLOGIES

These statements are essentially statements of belief, and reflect important cultural values as to the purposes of universities and academics. Cooke's statement does move us directly to the question of what research evidence supports the presumed or desired relationships. Only too often such statements on teaching and research ignore the considerable research and scholarly literature on this issue. (By 'research' in brief we mean some primary investigation and by 'scholarship' careful reflection on practice and review of the literature and research evidence: these definitions will be further explored in this chapter.)

Our standpoint is that as academics we cannot in good faith assert the value (of research and scholarship) to society and to our understanding and then fail to base our own practices on the research and scholarship of higher education. Thus, we argue that our policies and practices on teaching and research should stand on the research and scholarly evidence. (Hattie and Marsh, 1996 provide a superb meta-analysis of the research evidence at that time.)

However, as in other areas of enquiry, research does not provide a simple template for practice. We have to recognize that the concepts and definitions of 'teaching' and 'research' are themselves problematic, as are how one might define or measure 'quality' teaching or 'quality' research. The research on teaching–research relations varies as to how it conceives and models these relationships. Most studies assume that it is staff involvement in research that improves teaching, mainly through staff being involved in current debates in the discipline. Some studies and models have considered how staff involvement in teaching might improve research: for example by assisting academics to clarify their understanding of their research interests and develop new research areas.

In addition care has to be taken when drawing conclusions from studies using very different research methodologies, at different levels of analysis (the individual academic, the department, the institution, the (inter) national disciplinary community etc). We might presume that teaching–research relationships vary by issues of staff and student motivation and by academic level. Thus we might hypothesise that the relationships differ between, say, level one undergraduate courses and research components of taught postgraduate courses, a viewpoint that is clearly stated in the Robbins Report: 'in the graduate school there are no ultimate authorities, no orthodoxies to which the pupil must subscribe' (NCIHE, 1963). Most of the research has been at undergraduate level, for the assumption (which of course does need to be tested) is that at postgraduate level the connections are more self-evident (Clark, 1993a; Smeby, 1998). Also, we must be careful in taking research results from one type of institution (research led or access based, and so on) and from one national system and then extrapolating those results into different types of institutions and national systems.

Recognizing these caveats, research and scholarship does provide a strong coherent picture and one that can be applied to practice and policy.

INTERNATIONAL STATISTICAL EVIDENCE

Much of the research on teaching–research relationships has been statistical, often seeking to correlate measures of research productivity and student ratings of faculty and staff orientations to teaching and research at the level of the individual or the department. Much of this research is from the United States, though there have been related studies in both Australia and the UK.

In the UK there are strong positive correlations at a subject and department level between external national ratings of departments for teaching and research, that is Research Assessment Exercise (RAE) grades and Teaching Quality Assurance /Quality Assurance Agency ratings (TQA/QAA). This is often commented upon (for example, Cooke, 1998) and used to argue that good teaching is functionally dependent on high quality research by staff in that department. However, many would suggest that TQA/QAA grades in part reflect higher levels of resources in research based institutions or departments, and external perceptions of reputation forged in large measure through research. Even here, there are significant examples of departments that scored high on TQA and low on RAE (HEFCE, 1995; Hughes and Tight, 1995). There has been limited primary research on this issue, which is surprising given its salience to policy. A study by Entwistle (1995) in Scotland indicated that teaching quality assessors rated some departments as 'excellent' where they also noted that 'unimaginative teaching' prevailed. A comprehensive statistical analysis by Drennan and Beck (2000) clearly points to the positive effects on TQA scores of the academic standards of entering students, and levels of spending on computers and libraries: which of course say nothing directly about the impact of the college on student learning. This research reinforces but does not prove as a causal relation, the view that institutional research prestige, the age of the institution and its resources are giving 'halo effects' to perceived teaching quality. Furthermore, this close statistical interconnection in the UK between quality teaching and quality research does not mirror the available research in other national systems.

At the level of the individual, there have been extensive studies which demonstrate very low positive relations between measures of research productivity and student ratings of teaching. These are largely US studies and have been summarized in Pascarella and Terenzini (1991) and Terenzini and Pascarella (1994). Ramsden and Moses (1992) in a large Australian research study analysed teaching–research relationships at the level of the individual and at the level of the department across all subject areas, and concluded that 'there is no evidence in these results to indicate the existence of a simple functional relationship between high research output and the effectiveness of undergraduate teaching' (p 273). In a meta analysis of these correlation studies of university academics, Hattie and Marsh (1996) combined 58 research articles contributing 498 correlations and found no significant correlation between 'quality' in teaching and 'quality' in research (the overall correlation was 0.06). 'Based on this review we concluded that the common belief that teaching and research were inextricably intertwined is an enduring myth. At best teaching and research are very loosely coupled' (p 529). Perhaps one key factor here is staff time, and one might presume that time devoted to research would be at the expense of teaching (quality) and time spent on teaching would be at the expense of research. In their introduction to a later empirical study, Marsh and Hattie (2002) review the studies concerning time and research and teaching and conclude that 'those who spend more time in research do have higher research outcomes, but those who spend more time on teaching do not seem to be more effective teachers'. This review of that research literature was undertaken as part of a study of teaching–research relations in a large Australian research university. Using more recent multilevel statistical analysis they analysed the teaching effectiveness (based on student ratings) and research productivity of some 182 academics in a range of departments, and also how staff spent their time and their self-beliefs as to their abilities as teachers and researchers. They concluded:

> *Teaching effectiveness and research productivity are nearly uncorrelated, thus supporting the hypothesis that they are independent constructs* [ibid p 635]. Perhaps the major implication of this study is that it may be of most value to ask institutions is how they could re-weight research and teaching within institutions and departments. *A major aim would be to increase the relations between teaching and research and devise strategies to achieve this mission* [ibid 634; emphasis added].

At an institutional level, Astin (1993) and Astin and Chang (1995), in a study of 200 US four-year undergraduate colleges and using sophisticated measures of student development, concluded that 'a college whose faculty is research-orientated increases student dissatisfaction and impacts negatively on most measures of cognitive and affective development' (Astin, 1993: 363). The few institutions in this study that scored high on both 'teaching' and 'research' were rich, private colleges.

It was largely these statistical studies that caused one policy and funding orientated review of the research evidence to conclude that 'there is little functional interaction between undergraduate teaching and discovery research' (Ontario Council on University Affairs, 1994: 18). Similarly Gibbs (1995a: 148), reviewing this research evidence, argued that 'despite thirty years of research there is no support for the view or belief that quality in research is necessary or even supportive of quality in teaching'.

Others, we included, would see this research as indicating that these linkages are not 'automatic' and indeed that high levels of research output might have negative impacts on staff orientation to teaching. Thus Ramsden and Moses, in their conclusions to their empirical study at the levels of the individual and the academic department, point out that:

The findings are based on studies of association, rather than of functional mechanisms, and therefore cannot reveal the existence of a sequence of cause and effect....

It seems entirely plausible that heavy involvement in research and publication, at least for some academic staff and departments, take time and effort away from teaching undergraduates. However it is crucial to understand that *the present evidence in no way refutes the proposition that the continuing study of and intellectual curiosity about a subject is necessary for effective teaching. Our results indicate that the simple model of more research, therefore better teaching is suspect.*
(Ramsden and Moses, 1992: 292–93; emphasis added)

While such research should caution us as to seeing the relationship as being automatic or necessarily positive, further caution should be exercised on the policy conclusions drawn from this research. Further cautions include:

- Many of these studies reduce teaching and research quality to a single metric that makes little intuitive sense: is quality teaching for a large introductory course the same as for an advanced option?

- They seldom analyse the departmental, institutional and workload contexts in which staff and students are operating and which may be shaping the results they analyse.

- With significant exceptions the central focus of the studies has been at the level of the individual academic.

- Most of the studies are statistical studies of association, few are studies of causal relationships. More recent research has tried to move into these areas that are both difficult to research, but central to shaping policy and practice.

RECENT (QUALITATIVE) RESEARCH STUDIES

More recent, largely qualitative, research and scholarship on this question has developed findings and analyses that lend a greater complexity to the issue. They also indicate, even 'prove', that there can be positive features of the teaching–research nexus (including at undergraduate level).

Importance of course design

In a seminal article reviewing the then research evidence, Brew and Boud (1995a: 261) comment that these 'investigations of the links between teaching and research... have failed to establish the nature of the connection of the two.' They point to the limitations of much of this research, including an emphasis on correlation studies. They call for 'more fine grained studies' (p 272), focused on how academics experience teaching and research. They hypothesize that 'If there is a link between the two it operates through that which teaching and research have in common; both are concerned with the act of learning' (p 261).

While academics are not going to learn key pedagogical skills and attributes through doing subject-specific research, it can give them the experience of the process of 'deep' learning which then potentially can be communicated to students. They suggest that 'teaching and research are correlated when they are co-related' (ibid) and in conclusion suggest that one way of achieving this is to 'exploit further the link between teaching and research in the design of courses' (p 272). We will return to this theme in chapter 4.

Conceptions of teaching and research

Drawing on her recent research on academics' conceptions of research, Brew (1999: 299) argues that 'the relationships between teaching and research are dynamic and context driven'. The contexts include whether research is seen as an objective product or as a process of enquiry, and whether teaching is seen as transmission of what is known or an exploration. 'If researchers recognize the ways in which their activities parallel those of students and take steps to involve students in research-like activities, research can inform practice in facilitating learning' (Brew, 1999: 298; see also Brew, 2001b). Barnett, who in previous work had questioned the teaching–research nexus (see below), has now argued that universities need to be reformulated to help society deal with 'supercomplexity'. In this context, he argues that teaching and research:

> are activities (that) are separate and distinct and are not to be confused. However, research is a strong condition for teaching: being engaged in research of a frame-developing kind and projecting that research to wide publics is a strong – although not exactly necessary and certainly not sufficient – condition of teaching that is aimed at bringing about super complexity in the minds of students.... Institutions, but also their students, have a right to expect that their lecturers are engaged in research... *but the issue is whether lecturers adopt teaching approaches that are likely to foster student experiences that mirror the lecturers' experiences as researchers.*
> (Barnett, 2000: 163; emphasis added)

STUDENT PERCEPTIONS

Three linked research studies have demonstrated strong, positive student perceptions of staff research. Neumann (1994) interviewed a range of students from first-year undergraduates to postgraduates in a large Australian research university. Jenkins *et al* (1998) carried out focus group discussions with undergraduate students in a range of disciplines at Oxford Brookes. Both studies demonstrated positive student views of staff research. In these studies, student perceptions of staff involvement in research that was incorporated into their teaching, made students perceive their courses as up to date, stimulating intellectual excitement and giving the impression that staff was enthusiastic about what they were teaching. Staff integrating their research into their courses also gave students the opportunity to appreciate better the role of research in staff lives and the research role of the university. However both studies demonstrated that 'up-to-date knowledge and interest in the subject were not seen as substitutes for good teaching practice' (Neumann, 1994: 327). The Brookes study also revealed students wanted staff research (including absences on sabbatical and so on) to be better 'managed' so that the negative impacts, in particular staff not being available to students, were minimized.

A third study of student perceptions was carried out at the University of East Anglia (UEA) to in part examine the 'reality of University rhetoric... of the interaction of research and scholarship with teaching' (Zamorski, 2000: 5). Here the research project directors supervised students who were employed to research their learning experiences and those of their peers. They concluded that:

> Students value highly the experience of studying in a research environment but clearly there is a policy gap between policy intention and student perceptions at UEA. While students value being close to research, and to the idea of a university as a research community in which they are included, there are many ways in which they feel excluded.
> (Zamorski, 2000: 1)

A STRONGER POSTGRADUATE LINK

We have already demonstrated the widespread and common sense view that the teaching–research nexus is stronger at postgraduate level. However until recently little of the vast research on teaching–research relations had examined this issue. Given the worldwide growth of postgraduate courses, current research to guide practice and policy is of utmost importance. It is also relevant to point out that the 1963 UK Robbins Report's assumption of the central research focus of such courses may no longer apply. At that time, (postgraduate) higher education was clearly for an elite, many of whom then sought careers in academia, and theory and research-focused courses may have been appropriate. This may not necessarily be the case now. Much of the current growth in postgraduate courses is fuelled by students (many of them in professional careers) seeking training and qualifications to advance their careers outside academia.

A number of recent research studies clearly indicate the validity of this 'traditional' view of the 'research foundations' of postgraduate courses. Smeby (1998, 10) surveyed staff views on teaching–research relations at all four Norwegian universities and interviewed staff at Bergen and Oslo. He concluded that 'Very many teachers (thought their research influenced their teaching).... To a great extent at postgraduate level, while there were few who thought this at a lower level.' At Oxford Brookes we recently replicated the study of undergraduate student perceptions of (staff) research to a comparable group of postgraduate courses (see Lindsay, Breen and Jenkins, 2002). This research, albeit in one institution, demonstrated that:

- Both undergraduate and postgraduate students associate more benefits than disadvantages with lecturer research.

- While undergraduates did not see themselves as stakeholders in staff research, postgraduates did see staff involvement in research as of direct importance and value to them. However they did expect lecturer research to be directly 'salient', that is, relevant to *their* concerns.

- Postgraduate students make a greater number of positive statements, and a smaller number of negative statements about the effect of research upon teaching as the amount of research activity in their department increases.

STUDENT EPISTEMOLOGICAL DEVELOPMENT

Assisting students to develop sophisticated conceptions of knowledge and truth are at the core of what most of us assume to be the central intellectual goals of universities: and in Barnett's (2000) terms helping 'students cope with supercomplexity'.

Czaja Raukhorst and Baxter Magolda, in an as yet unpublished study (Baxter Magolda, 2001a) asked whether student involvement in research leads to epistemological development. Baxter Magolda is one of those researchers who have extended Perry's (1970) and other scholars' research on student intellectual development and conceptions of knowledge. Perry's research on a largely male sample of Harvard undergraduates 'described a progression of epistemic assumptions from knowledge as certain to partially uncertain to completely uncertain to relevant in context.... Relativistic thinking emerged with the realization that some knowledge claims are better than others and can be validated by evidence relevant to the context' (Baxter Magolda, 1999a: 40–41).

A major long term study of undergraduate student intellectual development by Baxter Magolda (1992: 75; see also Baxter Magolda, 2001b). revealed four ways of knowing:

> in absolute knowing students view knowledge as certain; their role is to obtain it from authorities. In transitional knowing students believe some knowledge is uncertain: their role shifts to understanding knowledge and finding processes to search for the truth. In independent knowing students believe most knowledge is uncertain and everyone has their own beliefs: their role is to think for themselves. In contextual knowing students believe that knowledge is constructed in a context based on judgement of evidence; their role is to exchange and compare perspectives, think through problems, and integrate and apply knowledge.
> (Baxter Magolda, 1992: 75)

Using this conceptual framework, Czaja Raukhorst and Baxter Magolda (Baxter Magolda, 2001a) undertook a study of the impact on students' conceptions of knowledge of a special summer ten-week independent research programme. (Such undergraduate research programmes are a feature of many US universities, and are analogous to the dissertation or thesis in the UK and elsewhere.) Students' perceptions of knowledge prior to, and on completion of, the programme were assessed and compared to those of a control group. (The central research tool was a 'measure of epistemological reflection' which involved students in writing a short essay that is then analysed for the nature of knowledge it reveals. Students doing the research programme, but not the control group, also kept a journal.) The central conclusions were that students who took part in the research programme became more confident as learners and more capable of thinking independently. These reports suggested that more complex assumptions of knowledge stemmed from participating in a mentored, independent research experience. Baxter Magolda (1999b: 9) sees such research as validating what she describes as 'constructive development pedagogy... [in which] teachers model the process of constructing knowledge in their disciplines, teach that process to students, and give students opportunities to practice and become proficient at it'. This research points us to the issues of course design we will explore in chapter 4.

In related research to that on the intensive research experience, Baxter Magolda (1999b: 29) analysed whether teachers using constructive development pedagogy could also have similar impacts on large classes and in 'content areas such as mathematics and science where subject mastery is vital'. She studied three different 'mainstream' courses where teachers were designing courses and teaching and assessing in ways that she considered would develop students as learners. Thus one was an advanced biology class where the teacher's goal was to 'help students think as scientists... identify useful questions, understand how to determine the next step in a research effort' (Baxter Magolda, 1999b:103), and whose pedagogy strongly featured a 'research project, presenting it in a scientific seminar format, and writing a grant proposal based on the paper' (p 128). The mathematics course was directed to 'help students understand that mathematical ideas and rules were created by humans and they, as humans, could participate in the creation process' (p 137), and the pedagogy was a very student centred investigative approach.

As well as her own observational judgements of these classes, and those of co-researchers, interviews with students and the 'measure of epistemological reflection', they tested students' conception of knowledge both early on in these courses and at the end. The results indicated significant intellectual growth for most students taking these courses.

We have described these studies by Baxter Magolda in some detail for the following reasons:

- They clearly point to the value of research based enquiries to student intellectual development, and to the centre of what many of us see as the central pedagogic focus of the university, that is, students developing more sophisticated levels of intellectual development.

- They offer very different research methodologies from most of the previous research that has questioned the value of research to student learning.

- Based as they are in Perry's (1970) work, they are situated in a research and scholarly literature that is generally positively received by those in organizations such as SEDA who have often questioned the value of discipline based research to student learning.

- They reinforce the arguments by Brew and Boud (1995a) for seeking the connections through seeing both teaching and research as 'learning' and in exploiting the links through course design.

VIEWS OF DEPARTMENT HEADS

Two linked studies, one by Neumann (1993a and b) in Australia, and the other by Rowland (1996) at Sheffield University, have demonstrated that department heads and administrators see strong positive connections between staff involvement in research and the intellectual currency of their courses. Rowland's respondents saw the connection as stronger in those staff whose teaching demonstrated an interactive approach and in particular those who conceived knowledge and research as being tentative and open to interpretation. Whilst there may be issues of self-interest in heads emphasizing the value of research (given its currency in departmental and institutional reputation), it also can be argued that they have in certain ways a more informed and sophisticated view as to what is teaching quality than is obtained by the many student questionnaire studies. Certainly their views and roles point us towards the issues we consider in chapter 6 about departmental organization to link teaching and research.

THE DISCIPLINARY ROLE

In both Neumann's (1993a and b) and Rowland's (1996) study of department heads, the discipline is seen as an important factor in shaping the relationship. A number of studies have further analysed these issues. Particularly in some of the sciences, staff research may be so far ahead of the undergraduate curriculum as to make strong connections between staff research and student learning very difficult (Ben-David, 1977; Jensen, 1998). In contrast, in the humanities the boundaries between 'original research' and 'scholarship' (see later discussion of 'scholarship') are seen as much more fluid and contested. There are also important differences in the use to which research is put; for example in health care the role of research in underpinning and examining professional practice needs to be central to both the pursuit and funding of research, and perhaps then to its role in the curriculum. In some professional disciplines such as planning (Griffiths, 2002) or engineering (Al-Jumailly and Stonyer, 2000), staff may have strong orientations and institutional requirements to consultancy. Perhaps in these disciplines the implications in such curriculum and departmental practice are for students to understand the research basis to consultancy and professional practice.

Colbeck (1998) carried out a detailed study of staff from English and physics from two contrasting US universities: one a high-prestige research university and the other a Masters-level university. In English, the linkage was stronger with respect to the *content* of the curriculum. In physics, the link lay more in the *process of inquiry* and the *involvement* of undergraduate and postgraduate students in staff research projects. This physics 'experience' gives empirical research evidence to Brew and Boud's (1995) view of the importance of course design.

The key role of the discipline in shaping the relationship, and the linked issue of how staff perceive both teaching and research, was a strong feature of research by Robertson and Bond (2001: 11) in exploring perceptions of teaching–research relationships among the staff at the University of Canterbury (New Zealand). Thus, for (some of) their interviewees 'in disciplines with a very hierarchical (knowledge) structure the relationship between teaching and research can only be activated at postgraduate level. These staff perceived that at undergraduate level students lacked the disciplinary framework to engage in inquiry.' (But see later discussion of this issue.)

WHAT 'COUNTS' AS 'RESEARCH'

Colbeck (1998) also shows that what 'counts' as research affects the possibility of staff seeing positive relationships between their involvement in research and their teaching, and possibly effecting their motivation to forge such links. At the high prestige university, for research funding and promotion what counted was high level, original research. Paradoxically, it was at the less well research-funded lower-level institution that staff saw stronger possibilities for linking teaching and research, because there, writing student textbooks, computer software and so on, could count as research. In the UK, Yorke (2000) has suggested that (discipline based) pedagogic research, which is perhaps not well supported by some departments and the Research Assessment Exercise (see later discussion), is one way of enabling staff to link teaching and research.

INSTITUTIONAL LEADERSHIP AND CULTURES

There has been little research on how institutional leadership, planning and culture shape the relationships, though the work of Colbeck, Rowland and Neumann shows that how teaching and research are conceived is critical (this research and these issues are explored in detail in chapter 5). Here it hopefully suffices to state that there are indications in some of the UK Audit Reports of institutions where some senior managers may not understand, and thus are unlikely to develop, the conditions that promote teaching–research links. The Audit of Exeter University stated:

The account argues strongly for the continuing and crucial value of the link between teaching and research; it acknowledges though that this relationship is more often assumed than explained. The audit team was told that this was a major question to be addressed, yet encountered staff that sometimes struggled to appreciate its significance. In practice, the precise relationship of the link between research and teaching seems not to have been addressed in any concerted way.
(HEQC, 1997: 3)

This sets up some of the issues we will explore in chapters 5 and 6, organizing the institution and the department to link teaching and research.

THE BOYER CRITIQUE

Some of the research and scholarly critiques of teaching–research relationships are in part, or in large measure, criticisms of the dominance of research in terms of its impact on institutional and individual prestige, in particular on what is seen as a lack of recognition of teaching in institutional and departmental planning and resourcing, and particularly in the lack of recognition to teaching in promotion decisions (for example, Gibbs, 1995b).

Particularly important here is the work of the late Ernest Boyer and his colleagues at the Carnegie Foundation in the United States (Boyer, 1990; Glassick, Huber and Maeroff, 1997; Rice, 1992; Hutchings and Shulman, 1999). Their work has had significant impacts on discussions of teaching–research relationships in mass higher education systems including in the UK and Australasia. They argue for a broader conception of 'scholarship' that values the various roles of universities and faculty. Boyer in *Scholarship Reconsidered* (1990: xii) argued that 'Research and publication have become the primary means by which most professors achieve academic status, yet many academics are drawn to the profession precisely because of their love for teaching or for service.' Boyer identified four separate but overlapping areas of scholarship:

- the scholarship of discovery research;

- the scholarship of integration, including the writing of textbooks;

- the scholarship of service, including the practical application of knowledge;

- the scholarship of teaching.

In parallel to the importance the Carnegie group have placed in the scholarship of teaching, work in the UK, in particular Elton (1992), Barnett (1992) and Healey (1999), has seen scholarship and the academics' knowledge of their discipline as a central responsibility of institutions and the system at large to support. Barnett (1992: 631) argues that:

> A genuine higher education today cannot be operated entirely separately from some kind of research base. But that does not mean that either institutions of higher education or their staff [are] obliged to conduct research. Staffs, though, do need to have the time and resources to keep up with their field of study so that they are immersed in its conversations. So *the argument here is not just theoretical: it has policy implications.*
> (Barnett, 1992: 631; emphasis added)

This argument for a more scholarly approach to teaching has shaped recent moves in the UK and elsewhere through organizations such as SEDA initially and now the Institute for Learning and Teaching (ILT) to professionalize teaching, to promote quality teachers (Gibbs, 1995a and b; Nicholls, 2001). It has also shaped the policy requirements and the financial inducements for institutions to create teaching and learning strategies and reward quality teaching (HEFCE, 1999).

BOYER AND LINKING RESEARCH AND TEACHING

Boyer offers a critique of how discovery research can devalue a concern for teaching. However his work can also be seen as a strong argument for encouraging, even requiring, a close linkage between (staff) research and undergraduate student learning. In *College* (Boyer, 1987), Boyer criticized the dominant passive lecture-based student experience, the separation of undergraduate education from enquiry or research process based teaching, and the lack of connections between research orientated staff and (undergraduate) student learning. Indeed much of the thrust of the powerful reform movement that stems from Boyer's and his colleagues' work is to bring a 'research as student' inquiry guided by (research based) staff ethos into the United States undergraduate curriculum. The 1998 Boyer Commission (http://notes.cc.sunysb.edu/Pres/boyer.nsf/), which was set up to promote implementation of Boyer's ideas into institutional planning in research universities, called for 10 key changes in undergraduate education, four of which directly address the teaching–research nexus, viz:

1. *Make research based learning the standard.* 'Learning is based on discovery based on mentoring. Inherent in inquiry-based learning is an element of reciprocity: faculty can learn from students as students are learning from faculty.'

2. *Construct an inquiry based freshman year.* 'The first year of a university experience needs to provide new stimulation for intellectual growth and firm grounding in inquiry-based learning and communication of information and ideas.'

3. *Build on the freshman foundation.* 'The freshman experience must be consolidated by extending its principles into the following years. Inquiry-based learning, collaborative experience, writing and speaking expectations need to characterize the whole of a research university education.'

4. *Culminate with a 'capstone experience'.* 'The final semester should focus on a major project and utilize to the full the research and communication skills learned in the previous years.'

To anticipate some of the accounts in chapter 5 of institutional policies, many of the research intensive United States universities, partly in response to Boyer and others, have responded by changing curricula and writing requirements, and there is some evidence that this has positively impacted on student 'learning productivity' (Kuh and Hu, 2001) and to ensuring that students benefit more from the university research environment. Book titles such as *Promoting Inquiry in Undergraduate Learning* (Weaver, 1989) and *Student Active Science* (McNeal and D'Avanzo, 1997) demonstrate this call to better connect (staff) research and student learning. Major research funders in the United States such as the National Science Foundation are requiring undergraduate student involvement as junior researchers in some competitive research awards to faculty. (See chapter 7.)

This US reform movement reinforces the importance placed by Brew and Boud (1995a) in getting academics to (re)-consider how they perceive teaching and research and the importance of course design (including methods of teaching and assessment) as ways to forge effective links between (staff) discipline based research and student learning.

Elton (2001: 43) has similarly argued that there 'may well be a positive link (between research and teaching) under particular conditions'. These he sees less in terms of the outcomes (for example, published papers of staff) that have been prominent in the research correlations studies, than in the extent to which students learn through some form of student-centred or enquiry-based approach, for instance, problem based learning (Savin-Baden, 2000). Brown and McCartney (1998: 126) come to similar conclusions in their review of the research evidence, as to the importance of staff enabling 'deep learning', where they advocate making 'courses (typically undergraduate courses) more like research'.

RESEARCH AND THE 'KNOWLEDGE ECONOMY'

Many of the recent national policies on higher education have focused on developing students with certain skills and orientations that will aid both their employability and national economic performance. The emphasis has largely been on certain 'key skills', such as teamwork. There is now a gathering body of argument (and perhaps evidence) that in the words of a recent Demos report, 'for the first time in history, knowledge is the primary source of economic productivity' (Seltzer and Bentley, 1999: 9). The emerging 'knowledge economy' is one that requires individuals with creativity and ability to develop, find and synthesize new knowledge. However, 'our educational structures are lagging behind.... The dominant educational paradigm still focuses on what students know, rather than how they use that knowledge' (ibid). If this is accepted, then students' understanding of the research process and ability to do research (and perhaps consultancy in some disciplines and professional areas) may be the vital key skill or knowledge the curriculum needs to develop.

This view is reinforced by the arguments of researchers such as Gibbons *et al* (1994) and Novotny *et al* (2000) that much knowledge, including how it is created and diffused, takes on the form of 'Mode 2 knowledge' where the boundaries between original research and application are much more messy and integrated. This suggests that, particularly in the professional areas of the university, there need to be strong continuities between research and teaching (Griffiths, 2002).

NATIONAL SYSTEMS AND POLICY IMPACTS

One of the reasons one has to be careful in taking research from one national context and applying it to another is that there may be important differences in how teaching and research are funded and audited, and how institutions and academics see their roles.

In the UK much university research is funded through the Research Assessment Exercise (RAE). Its purpose is to produce high quality research through competitively concentrating it in selected departments and institutions. It was not expressly designed to have any impact on teaching. However, research studies have shown that the RAE has had unintended consequences.

McNay (1998: 191) points to the fact that just as the UK HE system became a mass system, 'funding to academic staff to support their research was becoming more selective and exclusive' (see also Johnston, 1998). In a study commissioned by the Higher Education Funding Council (HEFCE) on the impact of the 1992 RAE on institutional and individual behaviour, McNay (1997a and b) used focus groups with staff and institutional managers, document studies and questionnaires to assess the impact of the RAE. McNay (1998: 196) in a later, non-official report, shows how the funding rewards the RAE offered led, at the level of the individual, the department and the institution, to 'a gradual separation, structurally of research from teaching'. Department heads reported that 'good researchers spend less time teaching... and more undergraduate teaching is done by part-timers and postgraduates' (McNay, 1998: 199).

Jenkins (1995a and b) in a study in geography, based on respondents in 14 anonymous departments, came to similar conclusions at undergraduate level. He also produced evidence to indicate that staffs in high ranking research departments were being withdrawn from writing educational software and textbooks, as this work did not 'count' in the RAE. Harley (2002: 198), in a study of the impact of the 1996 RAE on staff in sociology, psychology, marketing, finance and accounting in both pre- and post-1992 universities, showed a varied range of impacts, including 'the need to produce research in the new universities had in many cases resulted in conscious management strategy to divide academic labour into research active and non active, with those who were "non active" given more teaching'.

Yorke (2000) has argued that pedagogic research is devalued by the rules and values of the RAE as presently constituted. In particular, pedagogic research, which is based in the disciplines, is unlikely to be valued by the discipline-based panels. This is germane to this summary, for some see pedagogic research (Elton, 2001; Yorke, 2000) as *one* way effectively to link teaching and staff research. The potential role of pedagogic research in supporting the nexus is not developed further in this book.

There are scholarly studies of other related funding and audit systems that offer variations on the UK approach and suggest different ways of auditing teaching–research relationships. Woodhouse (1998: 39) reports on the system in New Zealand where the Academic Audit Unit (AAU) 'is required to audit not only the research policies and procedures of the university, but also how it links research and teaching, and the effect of this link'. Indeed following consultations with the universities the AAU Board determined that nationwide themes for audit in 2000–01 would be:

- 'provision and support for postgraduate students;

- the research–teaching link (at undergraduate, as well as at postgraduate level); and

- research policy, management and performance' (Meade and Woodhouse, 2000: 26).

Some of the research that is now coming from New Zealand universities suggests that this form of external audit is fostering a better awareness amongst academics of teaching–research relationships and perhaps strengthening the linkages (Robertson, 1999; Willis 2001).

Hong Kong recently changed its RAE system such that the 1999 RAE was designed to:

> enhance the understanding of the definition of research... to enlarge slightly the scope of the RAE to recognize other scholarship closely aligned to research, the Carnegie Foundation's definitions of research and research-related scholarly activities viz. the scholarship of discovery, application and teaching (Boyer, 1990) would be adopted. (French *et al*, 1999: 52) (http://ugc.edu.hk/english/documents/RAE99/raegn99f.html)

This discussion of the UK, New Zealand and Hong Kong systems for reviewing research performance clearly demonstrate the importance of considering how teaching–research relationships are shaped by national policies, issues that are further considered in chapter 7.

TEACHING–RESEARCH RELATIONSHIPS IN MASS HIGHER EDUCATION SYSTEMS

The discussion of the RAE and the work of Boyer raise the issue of what are the (appropriate) relationships between teaching and research in a mass higher education system; where universities are being restructured through globalization including the impact of information technology. Here the research and scholarly evidence does not provide a blueprint for policy. It does throw up theoretical and urgent policy concerns that impact at all levels of the system, down to the level of the individual academic.

In this context Barnett's (1992: 631) arguments have an added force: 'That does not mean that either institutions of higher education or their staff are obliged to conduct research.' One can readily see scenarios in which somewhere someone needs to be doing research, but that could be elsewhere in the world and perhaps outside academia. Curricular materials may be produced by a range of staff in a number of institutions and delivered globally to institutions where teacher-scholars support student learning. Such hypothetical scenarios have not been researched for their impact on teaching–research relationships. They are, though, the subjects of think tank style scholarly reports for individual institutions and national systems. See for example two Australian studies that try to chart the nature of academic work in the twenty-first century (Coaldrake and Stedman, 1999) and how the Australian system can develop a more diverse institutional base (Kemmis *et al,* 1999).

The Dearing Report on the future of UK Higher Education, (NCIHE, 1997) addressed the question of teaching–research relationships in a mass HE system, but also in an economy where research and research skills were seen as central to a new knowledge economy and society. Partly through a visit to the United States, Dearing was 'persuaded... of the important role of research and scholarship in informing and enhancing teaching' (para 8.7), and he recognized that 'there is a near universal rejection of the idea that some institutions of higher education should be teaching-only institutions' (para 11.60). However the report saw that 'to inform and enhance teaching' was but one of four roles and reasons for funding research in higher education.

Dearing further argued that the financial incentives for institutions to promote research were resulting, particularly in the ex-polytechnics and colleges, in staff doing research for which they 'may not have been trained and are not, in all cases, suited', and 'resulting in a downgrading of teaching' (para 11.63). Although Dearing's particular financial 'solution' to encourage some institutions to opt out of the RAE was immediately rejected by the UK higher education system, we should note the view that, for the Director of Policy for HEFCE, 'this was a serious proposal to tackle a serious problem' (Beckhradnia, 1998: 5).

IN CONCLUSION

Whether national policy makers in the UK and elsewhere are going to address directly those issues of funding, institutional diversity and the organization of funding and quality assurance remains to be seen. It is an issue that we will return to in chapter 7. In concluding this chapter we state the main conclusions we have reached on the basis of reviewing the research evidence.

For many academics there is a strong belief that quality teaching is functionally dependent on the lecturer being directly involved in research.

There is considerable research and scholarly evidence on teaching–research relations and as academics we should seek to build practice and policy on the basis of that evidence.

Much of the research and scholarly evidence demonstrates that the common academic belief of the teaching–research nexus is to be questioned. In particular many studies have analysed statistically the correlations between measures of teaching quality and research quality. The general conclusion one comes to from these studies is that 'the common belief that teaching and research were inextricably intertwined is an enduring myth. At best teaching and research are very loosely coupled' (Hattie and Marsh, 1996: 529).

However, to draw from this statistical evidence the conclusion, as did Gibbs (1995a: 148), that 'there is no support for the view or belief that quality in research is necessary or supportive of quality in teaching', also goes beyond the research evidence. *Mea culpa*; one of us (Jenkins, 2000a) used to share this interpretation of the research evidence. Even were that a valid interpretation of the research evidence, it leaves open whether (staff) research could be more effectively 'organized' to support student learning. This issue is particularly important, given, as we will show in chapter 3, that for many academics their motivation as a teacher is strongly linked to their interest in research.

More recent research (and scholarly discussions) on teaching–research relations has questioned the 'outcome' measures of teaching and research used in the quantitative correlative studies, and developed different qualitative and quantitative methods to analyse teaching–research relations. In particular they have built on the call by Brew and Boud (1995a: 272) for 'more fine grained studies', and their hypothesis that 'if there is a link between the two it operates through which teaching and research have in common; both are concerned with the act of learning' (p 261).

Much research scholarship and research on teaching–research relations has opened up the complexity of the issues: including the level at which students are studying; how they are taught and assessed; the discipline, and how staff commitments to developing the link may be shaped by institutional and national reward and funding systems.

Also, the more recent research does point clearly to the (potential), and we believe the importance, of (staff) discipline based staff research to student learning. Such research has included focus group and interview based studies of student perceptions, and perhaps more significantly research on how student involvement in research can support their developing more sophisticated and advanced conceptions of knowledge.

Perhaps paradoxically, much of this research shifts some or many of the implications for policy and practice away from staff as researchers and towards students as learners. Elton (2001: 43) argues that 'a positive research and teaching link primarily depends on the nature of the students' learning experiences, resulting from appropriate teaching and learning processes, rather than on particular inputs or outcomes'. That is why we give such emphasis to what those learning experiences could be, by setting out in chapter 4 strategies for designing courses to maximize the potential valued linkages between teaching and research.

However, to us, the research evidence reported in this chapter also shows the importance of the 'inputs', in particular how staff are organized and supported (including issues of how departments, institutions and national systems conceive the roles of higher education and how they organize, appraise and 'reward' teaching and research). These issues then are developed in chapters 5–7 regarding departmental, institutional and national organization.

To reinforce the argument in chapter 1, the word 'reshaping' in the book's title brings out our conclusion, that if we value the link then it needs 'creating', 'designing', by a whole range of 'actors', levers and levels in the higher education system.

But before we consider how to act to develop effective linkages in these areas, we turn to the research and scholarly evidence on student and staff motivation and teaching–research relations, for that evidence sets up issues that need to be recognized in strengthening the links. Such evidence further ensures that we base policy and practice more firmly on research evidence, because we see that as what should be one of the central characteristics of higher education.

However, in the final analysis our views and actions on teaching–research relations are in part (or even large measure) about what we see as the pedagogic purposes and roles of universities and academics in society. We do see those roles as centrally concerned with helping students and society to value and understand knowledge obtained through research, and help bring about what Barnett (2000: 163) calls 'supercomplexity' in the minds of students'. We now turn to student (and staff) motivations.

3

Academic research and student motivation in higher education

From my point of view, there would be absolutely no point in doing the course if the people who are teaching on it didn't have a really high and active research profile.
(Anthropology student)

I find the lecturers that I assume are doing the research more vibrant and excited about what they're trying to impart.
(Education student)

I think, a lot of the time it's been their enthusiasm for their own research that's come across in particular lectures, and that's sort of sparked me off.... I think certainly that's one of the factors that's perhaps directed some of the research that I've done, has been the enthusiasm that I've gained from a particular lecturer or something.
(Education student)

You also need the research to be at the cutting edge, because there's no point in doing a course to find that it's outdated when you get in the real world.
(Biology student)

I had the feeling that I've been one step further than the people who have got the book, or the people who have just access to the book, which was a great feeling. It was probably the only time in the courses that I got this feeling, like, 'Oh, great! My supervisor, this teacher has put us before the others, so we are... even... yeah, one-step ahead.'
(Hospitality Management student)

These are some fairly typical comments made by undergraduate and post-graduate students about the impact upon their own experiences of research that was carried out by their lecturers (Jenkins *et al*, 1998; Lindsay, Breen and Jenkins, 2002). All of these comments concern effects on motivation, and this is a strong indication that engagement in research has a major impact upon the way the people who support their learning are perceived and responded to by students. The rest of this chapter explores the evidence for believing that lecturer research affects student motivation, the nature of the effects, and how the effects can be used to support student learning more effectively.

CENTRAL THEMES

This chapter is divided into three parts: all are concerned with the relationship between lecturer research activities and motivation, but the first two parts focus on the impact of research on student motivation and how student motivation can be enhanced through research, whereas the third part considers how involvement in research is related to motivation amongst lecturers themselves.

In connection with student learning, 'motivation' is the word generally used to refer to those inner processes that determine whether learners will engage in a task, the amount of effort they will expend, the length of time they will persevere and the persistence they will show when obstacles are encountered. Motivation is a central (research) concern of psychologists, and this chapter draws on that work and asks you the reader to appreciate its particular language and insights. For those who seek to facilitate learning, as for those who would manage any human activity, motivation is of paramount importance (Pajares, 1996).

It is thought too often that motivation is a problem in education, but not in higher education. Motivating students is something schoolteachers need to do, but lecturers do not. Students choose to enter higher education so they are responsible for their own learning. Lecturers provide the water; students must decide for themselves whether to drink. These views are increasingly hard to defend. Opening up higher education has drawn in students who are less well prepared and more uncertain about their goals: and in the particular context of this book perhaps less motivated by research. Poorly motivated students often drop out, and departments and universities are judged by performance indicators such as 'wastage' rates. Higher student:staff ratios means less contact with lecturing staff and a more urgent need to facilitate autonomous learning. If lecturers do attend to student motivation they are likely to see results such as higher levels of student satisfaction, lower rates of failure, less dependence on hard-pressed lecturers and better quality learning. Motivation can only be ignored when it can be taken for granted, or when learning outcomes are of no consequence.

THE IMPACT OF RESEARCH ON STUDENT MOTIVATION

Linked research studies

A series of research studies on the impact of lecturer research on student learning was initiated at Oxford Brookes in 1995. The results seem to be quite systematic, and to suggest that lecturer research is, generally speaking, positively valued by students and perceived by both undergraduate and postgraduate students to have beneficial effects on their learning (Jenkins *et al*, 1998; Lindsay, Breen and Jenkins, 2002). (See also the previous discussion in chapter 2 where this research was but part of the wider issue of student perceptions of (staff) research.)

Both undergraduates and postgraduates think that research activity makes their lecturers more enthusiastic, increases their credibility, and ensures that their knowledge is up to date. They also think that involvement in research means that lecturers are less accessible, and can sometimes lead to curriculum bias if narrowly focused research is given too much attention.

While both undergraduates and postgraduates agree about the generic benefits of lecturer involvement in research, postgraduates also apparently *expect* the lecturers who support their learning to be involved in research; and they insist that this research should be relevant to the content of their courses. In one study for example, out of eight different university departments, there was only one case in which the frequency of negative comments about research outweighed those that were favourable, and interestingly this was the department that received the lowest external RAE rating in the sample.

Given that the undergraduate and postgraduate student samples were drawn from the same eight disciplines, the differences between them in attitudes to research suggest immediately that motivation is involved. To put it crudely, undergraduates are seeking to extend their education, and they expect the people who teach them to capture their interest, to present current knowledge, and to speak authoritatively within their discipline. The great majority of postgraduates also have more specific goals: either they want to become researchers themselves (requiring knowledge of current research issues and mastery of relevant methodologies), or they want to acquire knowledge that can be applied in some professional or commercial context (requiring knowledge currency and experience of the contexts of application). The more specific expectations about lecturer research reported by postgraduates are clearly related to the more specific goals by which they are motivated.

Student goals

Research studies investigating student motivation have confirmed that attitudes towards research activity in their department are strongly influenced by the goals that students are pursuing (Breen and Lindsay, 1999; Lindsay, Breen and Jenkins, 2002). Amongst undergraduates *'intrinsic motivation'* and a specific form of *'course competence'* are associated with positive attitudes to departmental research activity while *'extrinsic'*, *'social'* and *'achievement'* motivations are not. Amongst research students and Masters students, positive attitudes towards research are associated with an orientation towards acquiring theoretical knowledge for the purpose of 'developing one's potential', attaining 'freedom at work', becoming involved in 'interesting' and 'creative work', 'influencing society' and 'achieving important things' in professional practice. Motivations that are not associated with positive attitudes to research tend to emphasize the obtaining of qualifications, or establishing a successful or a secure career without any reference to the acquisition of knowledge.

Disciplinary variations

As well as varying with motivation, student attitudes to research by their lecturers are also affected by academic discipline. For example, Breen and Lindsay's (1999) data suggest that positive student attitudes and motivations can be enhanced by interactions between undergraduates and faculty that employ or concern shared beliefs and values derived from the discipline. Lindsay, Breen and Jenkins (2002) found that *hard-pure-life* type disciplines (for instance, biology) have more positive attitudes towards research than *applied* disciplines. Several of the Oxford Brookes investigations noted a consistently negative attitude towards research among business administration students. Jenkins *et al* (1998) suggest that this could result from an inappropriately narrow conception of research ('ivory-tower', 'blue skies', 'theoretical' and so on), and certainly the meaning of 'relevant research' can shift dramatically between for example, sciences, humanities and applied disciplines.

Amount of research

The amount of research going on in a department might be expected to affect the impact of lecturer research activities on student learning. Using RAE rating as a proxy for the quantity of research Lindsay, Breen and

Jenkins (2002) reported a clear relationship between student views on the value of lecturers' research, and the RAE rating of their department. The higher the RAE rating, the more positive comments students made about the way research affected their learning. Amongst undergraduates, the number of negative comments also increased with RAE score. Postgraduates however said less negative things about research as RAE ratings went up. This pattern of results can be explained by the following assumptions:

- Both groups of students value research by staff because it enhances enthusiasm, credibility, currency etc.

- A high level of research activity in a department will increase student awareness of ongoing research and its impact upon teaching, and students will be more likely to have positive comments to make.

- For undergraduates, negative features of lecturer research activity (reduced access and availability etc) are also likely to become more evident as the amount of research activity in a department increases, leading to more negative comments.

- Postgraduates are more likely to be involved in lecturer research and to see direct benefits for their own learning. They are less likely to experience reduced access because of different patterns of contact (eg longer teaching year, small group or one to one supervision etc). Hence more research leads to fewer negative comments.

A single picture

If these variables are put together into a single picture it is clear that the question of how research by lecturers interacts with student motivation is complex and subtle:

- Students as a whole seem to prefer to learn from staff who are involved in research.

- Students who are motivated to seek knowledge, value research activity more than those who seek qualifications.

- Students in disciplines organized around a cumulative knowledge base (for instance, biology) are more likely to value research than those from disciplines based on the application of softer and more transient knowledge (for instance, business administration).

- Postgraduates are more likely than undergraduates to see themselves as stakeholders in lecturer research, and are less likely to perceive negative effects.

- Students value research activity, but as its impact upon them increases, undergraduates become increasingly aware of downside effects while postgraduates do not.

In the rest of this part of the chapter, we shall be suggesting ways in which research activity can be used to enhance student motivation, and ways in which student motivation can be used to assist them to gain benefit from lecturer research activities, and to reduce negative impacts. The reader should continue to bear in mind the important differences within the student population that have been summarized here.

Though most of the following discussion focuses on the impact of lecturer research on student motivation to learn, other effects of such research upon student motivation are also important. Quality impressions of universities among academics and others who advise students are often influenced by reading or hearing about research activity. It is therefore likely that directly or indirectly, student motivation to apply to an institution is affected by the quantity and quality of its research achievements. Once embarked on a programme of studies, students certainly report that their opinion of the course and its staff, and their pride in being a member of a particular department are influenced by its research reputation.

POTENTIAL IMPACTS

With respect to student learning, lecturer research activity has the potential for impacting in both a positive and a negative way upon student motivation. Potential positive effects on student motivation can occur via the following effects of research activity on lecturer performance (Brew and Boud, 1995b; Jenkins *et al*, 1998):

- enhancing lecturer motivation;
- increasing lecturer enthusiasm;
- deepening lecturer knowledge;
- broadening lecturer skills;
- increasing lecturer confidence;
- increasing lecturer credibility;
- providing practical examples;
- supplying textual or visual resources.

Unfortunately, the list of potential negative effects of lecturer research on student motivation is not much shorter (Ramsden and Moses, 1992; Astin, 1993; Jenkins *et al,* 1998) and includes:

- reducing lecturer preparation time;

- reducing availability to students;

- substitution by less experienced staff;

- biasing teaching towards personal expertise;

- poor tolerance of alternative viewpoints;

- pitching classes at too high a level.

Developing appropriate strategies

This chapter now develops from two important assumptions: first, positive effects of lecturer research on student motivation will only occur as a result of an appropriate strategy, and second, negative effects of lecturer research on student learning will only be prevented as a result of an appropriate strategy.

This section begins by very briefly reviewing some important concepts and distinctions, which are essential to understanding the interaction between student learning and motivation. It then offers practical suggestions as to how research can be used to enhance student motivation in ways, which should benefit learning.

Motivation is related to learning in three important ways. First, learning requires effort and people only expend effort when they are compensated by some benefit. (Sometimes people do come to learn for the pleasure of learning itself, but this is unusual and there is little need to worry about motivation in such cases.) Second, people generally learn so that they can do something better in the future, because the motivation for learning is usually a desire to improve at something other than the learning itself. Third, some aspects of motivation (such as fear of failure, and anxiety to succeed) disable rather than facilitate learning. From the triarchic relationship between learning and motivation come three general principles which underlie the management of learning:

Make learning rewarding
Learning can be made rewarding by the use of cognitive variables, such as interest, curiosity and positive feedback, by the use of affective variables such as surprise and humour, or by the use of social variables such as approval and group membership.

Discover learner goals
If you know what learners are trying to achieve, then you can give them feedback that is meaningful in terms of progress towards their objectives (avoiding reactions such as 'I know my coursework marks are good, but is this really helping me to become a teacher, architect etc?').

Minimize obstacles to learning
The two most common barriers to learning are:

Affect barriers
These arise when learners' emotional needs are not met within the learning situation, for example when they are excessively anxious, when they will not try for fear of failing to meet their own (or others') standards, or when they fear being shown up as inferior to other learners.

Conceptual barriers
These usually arise when students enter the learning context with faulty preconceptions, or when they try to understand new material in terms of inappropriate models. Learning is often not just a process of filling an empty vessel, but involves amending or dislodging existing belief content (Strike and Posner, 1985; 1992).

Learning to know and learning to do

Psychologists have constructed a formidable body of knowledge about the cognitive processes that support learning. We shall focus here only on two important distinctions (Searleman and Herrmann, 1994). Later we will show how this knowledge can support staff in linking student motivation to research.

Declarative (versus procedural) memory
This is where propositional knowledge (such as 'birds lay eggs') is stored. The contents of declarative memory are available to consciousness and consist of such things as facts and images. People are aware of what they know and can report it to others. Procedural memory stores action routines and motor programmes. The knowledge underlying driving a car, typing a sentence, or walking across a room is procedural. It underlies action and skilled performance.

Semantic (versus episodic) memory
Declarative memory seems to be subdivided into two components (Tulving, 1985). Semantic memory is where we store our knowledge of abstract timeless meanings and conceptual relationships, such as the knowledge

that 'light is a form of energy' and 'monarchs have power over commoners'. Episodic memory is where we store our knowledge of events that happen to us ('episodes') such as memories of social activities, and things we have done or dreamt.

The importance of these constructs is that different learning strategies are necessary to enter material into each of the memory subsystems, and which strategy is chosen depends upon the way the learning environment is structured and upon learner beliefs about the conditions under which retrieval is likely to occur.

Theories of motivation

Probably the single most influential view of motivation is Maslow's (1970) view that people have a hierarchically ordered set of needs that determine the behaviours they are motivated to carry out. The highest priority group of needs are deficiency needs: physiological needs must be satisfied before safety needs emerge, then belongingness and love needs become dominant, and finally esteem needs. When deficiency needs are satisfied, growth needs emerge: the need to know and understand, aesthetic needs, and finally self-actualization needs. Maslow's theory reminds us that student learning may be catastrophically disrupted by the consequences of poverty (Lindsay and Paton-Saltzberg, 1995), domestic violence, failed relationships or feelings of rejection. It also suggests that intrinsic motivation (associated with growth needs) emerges only when deficiency needs are satisfied. Theories that treat motivation as a dimension of personality, such as achievement orientation (McClelland *et al*, 1953; Entwistle and Ramsden, 1983), are of academic interest but rather less practical utility. Universities cannot exclude intellectually capable candidates on the basis of their personality, and lecturers cannot set out to manipulate personality in the name of teaching.

A more powerful approach is the view that motivation is rooted in cognition. There are numerous variations on cognitive explanations of motivation, which include social cognitive theory, 'theories about self-concept, and attributions of success and failure, expectancy-value, goals, self-schemas and possible selves' (Pajares, 1996). For present purposes we do not need to choose between them, noting only that they are all broadly in agreement that learner goals (what they intend to do) and learner beliefs are of key importance – particularly beliefs about the difficulty of a task, its relevance to their personal goals, and beliefs about their own competence in the task domain (self-efficacy). A further aspect of cognition which can have a profound influence upon motivation to learn and perform is control, emphasized in the theory of learned helplessness (Seligman, 1975), in Rotter's ideas about locus of control (Rotter, 1982) and in Bandura's views about self-efficacy (Pajares, 1996). Very briefly, Seligman's theory is that if a task environment produces negative outcomes regardless of what learners do, they may learn not to learn, because what they do makes no difference. Rotter suggests that people develop relatively long term expectations about the extent to which they can influence events: people with an internal locus of control believe that what they do makes a considerable difference to the outcomes they experience. People with an external locus of control believe that what happens to them is largely outside their control. Similarly, Bandura (1977) argues that personal beliefs about self-efficacy have a major impact upon what challenges learners will take on and persist at. All three theories make the point that motivation to learn in a current learning situation may be considerably affected by the legacy of earlier learning experiences.

Approaches to learning

Marton and Saljo (1976) gave students lengthy academic articles to read and subsequently asked them about their approach to the task and their understanding of the content. Marton and Saljo found that some students took a 'deep approach', characterized by personal involvement with the task, seeking to extract the underlying meaning and forming connections with prior knowledge and other contexts. Other students took a 'surface approach', seeking to remember rather than understand, forming superficial connections between task elements, and few or no connections at all with knowledge from outside the immediate task. Entwistle and Ramsden (1983) have also claimed that there is an 'achieving approach' characterized by highly organized strategies for gaining good grades, rather than seeking to learn to gain understanding. These approaches to learning are not related in any simple way to student ability, though they are likely to affect academic performance. The important point is that the learning environment appears to play a large part in determining the approach that students take to learning. Lecturers must remain constantly alert to the fact that they are not only providing learners with what is to be learnt, they are also giving cues which influence student choices about how to approach learning. For example heavy workloads assessed by multiple choice examinations will predispose towards a surface approach. Moderate workloads and the use of problem based learning are more likely to foster a deep approach (Johnston, 2000).

MOTIVATION IN PRACTICE: CREATING LINKAGES WITH RESEARCH

Making explicit *personal* conceptions of learning

Learning is not a given, so lecturers need to make explicit their own conceptions of learning. If they do not, students will hunt for cues as to what is required and often arrive at wrong conclusions. There is rarely any good reason to risk misdirecting students about what they should be trying to learn. Most lecturers see research activity as an important arena in which they themselves learn. This means that they are in a good position to share learning experiences with students, and to project themselves as fellow learners rather than as 'experts' talking down to 'novices'. Researchers are in a good position to serve as models of learners who seek understanding for its own sake, and knowledge as an intrinsic good. The evidence is overwhelming that students who adopt this deep approach are more successful at learning, and their higher motivation makes them more likely to discuss their work outside classes, to undertake course related work and activities, and to read textual material which is additional to that prescribed.

Exploring *student* conceptions of learning

If learners expect passive learning via lectures they are likely to react negatively to such activities as group work and problem based learning (and vice versa). It is important to share expectations and try to achieve a match between teacher and learner goals. Discussion of personal research activity can be a good basis for this kind of expectation matching. Very little research activity is carried out with the aim of allowing someone to do well in tests. Almost invariably it is aimed at enhancing understanding or producing some definite beneficial outcome. Giving students insight into the reasons a lecturer values knowledge is a good start in shifting them towards the same values, or at least in causing them to question their own instrumentalism and short-termism.

Responding to student *needs*

Most students, particularly younger ones, need to feel liked, and to receive approval, support and respect. Discussing personal research shifts dialogue from public epistemological space into the lecturer's own back garden. It is a safe form of disclosure, and disclosure increases trust and intimacy. Discussion of personal research can provide an excellent opportunity to learn students' names, to discover their interests, to communicate confidence in their ability, and to indicate that their values and ideas are respected.

Using *non-verbal* communication channels

Learners are greatly affected by the emotional messages that lecturers transmit. Enthusiasm is one of the features of lecturer style which students emphasize as most important in promoting effective learning. It is one of nine dimensions of teaching effectiveness that have been identified consistently in more than 30 published factor analyses of student evaluations of teaching (Marsh and Roche, 1997). Students often perceive enthusiasm as being a consequence of involvement in research, though this is evidently not a necessary genesis. Certainly, it is highly likely that active researchers will be enthusiastic about their own research domain, and sharing this enthusiasm appears to have a considerable and positive impact on student learning and perceptions of lecturer effectiveness.

Discovering learner *goals*

Students are often motivated to learn because of what the resulting knowledge or qualification enables them to do. Involvement in research usually gives insights into how knowledge can be used and sometimes into what qualifications are important for what career paths. Find out why students are taking your course, why they want to gain the degree towards which it counts. The more you know about their motivations, the easier it is to create links with learning. Your experience of the utility of the knowledge they are seeking to acquire will raise the value that students assign to it.

Establishing what learners want to *know*

To retain knowledge long term, and to keep it available for flexible use, learners must incorporate it into more or less permanent memory structures. They will only choose, and make the effort, to do this if they believe the knowledge will be important or useful in the post-assessment future. Explaining why knowledge is useful and what it is useful for not only motivates students to learn, but also further increases the probability that they will take a deep approach to learning.

Making learning *interesting*

Researchers have already gone through the process of justifying their work and setting it in a practical or economic context. 'Interest' comes from forming links to pre-established prioritizations built into a learner's cognitive system. The kinds of thing that capture interest – and interest means focused attention, resistance to distraction and relatively effortless learning – include linking knowledge to the real world; setting puzzles; introducing humour; springing surprises; relating learning content to social success, mating and reproduction, death and disaster: universal themes and objectives which readily capture the human imagination. Researchers have usually already made the links, heard the jokes, and played the games. Use this experience to help students learn.

Finding out what learners want to *do*

Remember that learners will want to do something with knowledge beyond reproducing it in assessments. Besides using it to get a job, many students will learn more effectively if they know the specific powers to act appropriately that a body of new knowledge confers. Try to use research experience to relate knowledge to action contexts in which it will be used.

Making learning *relevant*

Everyone agrees that making learning relevant is a good thing. But relevance is not intrinsic to particular bodies of information, it is goal-dependent. You can only make relevance connections to help someone learn if you know what learners intend to do with the knowledge or skills that they acquire. Researchers already know many ways in which knowledge can be used, so if they find out what students are aiming to do they can often explain how course-related knowledge can help. Creating new motivations is difficult; relating new knowledge to pre-existing motivations is much more likely to be a success.

Recognizing motivational diversity

Students are a diverse group, and they obviously do not all share identical motivational profiles. Nevertheless, a relatively small set of motivations does frequently recur among students. Some of the most common are:

- wanting to enhance employability via qualifications;
- wanting to enhance self-efficacy through acquiring knowledge and skills;
- wanting to succeed within a competitive assessment regime;
- wanting to master a discipline/body of knowledge (physics, English and so on);
- wanting to please or impress others (parents, teachers and so on);
- wanting to learn for its own sake;

- wanting to play a role (student, engineer and so on);

- wanting to belong to a group (the university, the department, a coterie).

Any reasonably large class will include most of these subtypes, as well as every imaginable combination of them. As it is impractical to analyse the motivational make-up of each student and then to provide a tailor-made course version, a sensible alternative is to try to offer something for everyone. Use your research experience to consider how knowledge and skills in your course can assist students in satisfying these motivations. Then use problem solving exercises, examples, illustrations or case studies to help make the payoffs explicit. (For instance, point out how course knowledge will help in the research environment or the world of work, what new skills can be used to accomplish that and make it clear when you are pleased or impressed with a student's work.)

Encouraging *appropriate* types of learning

Do not assume that 'surface learning' is always bad (terminology and vocabulary often need to be learnt by rote), or that deep learning is always good (conceptual links established within an unfamiliar domain by novice learners will often produce misconceptions, deep learning is often irrelevant for procedural memory: skills just need practice). Do consider the type of learning which is most appropriate for content, learner and likely retrieval conditions. As a general rule surface learning is usually necessary early in a course to establish essential cognitive foundations. Move to a pattern of course organization that encourages deep learning as early as possible. Deep learning is encouraged by:

- relatively light workloads;

- learning tasks and assessments requiring comprehension rather than memory;

- belief among learners that knowledge will be useful beyond the demands of assessment;

- confidence that the knowledge being acquired is valid and applicable outside the immediate learning context.

Research experience can be used to assist in implementing most of these course features.

Establishing *communicator* credibility

Deep learning occurs when a student chooses to expend effort to change the organization and content of their long-term memory. Students will only make this choice if they think knowledge is unequivocally valid, and that it will be valuable in the future and across a broad range of contexts. Motivating students to make this choice is a critical aspect of learning facilitation. Modifying permanent memory on the basis of word-of-mouth communication is an act of trust, which albeit usually in a modest way, changes the learner's characteristics as a rational agent. The teacher role-label is not always enough to confer sufficient trust to achieve this. It is helpful in establishing trust if teachers are able to present expertise credentials, for example cases in which they have participated in collecting or interpreting evidence through research, or contexts in which they have used or applied knowledge in the context of consultancy. It is obviously possible to achieve the same credibility through displaying scholarship, but students do seem to react very positively to evidence that the teacher is more than just a retailer of knowledge. Credibility establishment presents an important opportunity to use research experience to benefit teaching.

Using *experiential learning*

The evidence is overwhelming that learning through doing is far more effective than learning through being told. Three obvious reasons are that that action is a multi-sensory experience, that in doing learners directly discover the utility of knowledge, and that in seeing that knowledge works, the student is relieved of the necessity to take someone else's word for it. Consider how experiences you have undergone as a researcher can be used to construct exercises that permit students to learn through discovery.

Establishing *evaluator* credibility

Students are likely to rely upon feedback only if they think it is valid and fair. Experiences as an academic researcher can often be used to help convince students that your opinion is authoritative on matters such as: writing essays and reports, oral presentations, evaluating evidence, testing hypotheses and critiquing the work of others.

Investigating prior *misconceptions*

Often a learner needs to change existing beliefs. Lecturers cannot assume that students are 'greenfield sites'. However, learners will not be motivated to change their current conceptual framework unless they are persuaded, first that the framework is defective, and second that a superior alternative is available. This may sound reminiscent of how theoretical change occurs in science, and indeed it is helpful to see this process as similar to establishing new knowledge through research. The knowledge community has pre-existing beliefs that must be identified and shown to be inadequate before change is likely to occur. In science this is often achieved by testing hypotheses to compare new and old theories. The research process can be used as a guiding model in understanding how to bring about conceptual change in individuals.

Controlling *over-motivation*

Often students become too focused on achievement, too competitive in outlook, or too obsessive about assessment. Any of these behaviours is likely to produce debilitating anxiety. In such circumstances the last thing students need is further motivating. Anxiety symptoms compete for attention, distract from learning cues, impair memory processes and disrupt physical and verbal performance. Sensible principles to control the impact of anxiety are to limit the use of competitive tasks and to avoid forcing anxious students to make group presentations. More benign learning exercises are those that encourage students to work cooperatively with others in teams, which foster learning through discovery, and which allow students to learn at their own rate. Again, research activities often constitute a rich source of ideas and tasks for learning of this kind.

Dealing with the *threat of failure*

Some students prefer not to try rather than risking 'failure'. Try to boost their confidence through using tasks at which they succeed. This often requires finding a delicate balance between challenge and threat (too easy demotivates through lack of challenge; too difficult becomes threatening). Emphasize learning rather than performance goals by explaining that all learning is a form of success, but learning cannot occur without negative feedback from performance. Research experience is often helpful as a basis for knowing how challenging tasks can be. It is also an excellent source of examples to illustrate points such as, setbacks are not evidence of personal inadequacy, and falsifying a favourite theory can be more informative than generating redundant confirmatory evidence. It is often helpful to actively maintain student awareness that learning is occurring, for example by getting students to keep a learning diary or similar record of progress.

Allowing learners to *succeed* in some activity

Do not risk fostering 'learnt helplessness' by unintentionally communicating that the teacher is always right and the student is inevitably wrong. Give learners a chance to do things successfully so as to enhance their feelings of self-efficacy. You need tasks that you know will work. Research problems that you have already solved, or that you know how others have solved, are often a far better source of learning materials than artificial exercises, and they also provide an opportunity for lecturers to discuss their research ideas, demonstrate enthusiasm and so on.

Transferring *control* to learners

Expert performance requires learners to be in control of events rather than reacting to them. In learning to fly a plane, there is a moment when quite literally, control is handed to the learner. In most learning situations the transfer of control is more gradual and less overt. The experience of being in control is itself a powerful motivator, so give students as much control as possible, as early as possible. This may involve modest delegation of control such as allowing students to choose tasks or topics, the order of events, or the way the social situation is structured. More advanced and more valuable exercises involve initiating students directly into the process of knowledge creation by allowing them to originate research ideas and design studies that test or implement them. The designs might then form the basis for critical discussion or be carried out as project work. It hardly needs saying that the skills involved in facilitating student work of this kind are in very large part those of the researcher.

Sharing evaluation criteria with learners

A key element in the control transfer process is the mastery of evaluation criteria. To sustain motivation, learners need positive feedback indicating that they are succeeding. In the early stages of learning this usually comes from a teacher, because for learning to be autonomous it must start to come from the task. Learners cannot identify successful performance until they have mastered an appropriate set of evaluation criteria. Giving away the mysteries of evaluation is an essential stage in the process of handing over control.

Recognizing the critical importance of feedback

Feedback is one of the most important tools for enhancing and sustaining motivation that is under lecturer control. Feedback should be presented as soon as possible after performance has been evaluated. It should be provided as often as is practicable, it should be readily interpretable and as precise as possible. Vagueness and ambiguity should be minimized, and feedback should whenever possible apply to local performance on a learning task, rather than consist of global judgements about a learner. Feedback should emphasize positive features of learning, rather than negative features.

ACADEMIC RESEARCH AND LECTURER MOTIVATION

> The opportunity to do research is an important reason why people decide on an academic career.
> (Higher Education Funding Council for England, 2000 a: 4)

We now briefly consider the issue of how involvement in research is related to motivation amongst lecturers themselves.

Lecturer motivation and teaching quality

The most important issues associated with lecturer motivation from the viewpoint of a university concerned to maximize the quality of student learning, are the ability of the university to:

- recruit high quality lecturing staff;
- retain lecturing staff once recruited;
- maintain the quality of lecturing staff through training and development;
- ensure that lecturing staff are committed to teaching quality;
- provide appropriate resources such as time and facilities.

Lecturer motivation and academic research

Engagement in academic research impacts upon each of these motivational issues in fundamental ways. Recruitment is affected because high quality subject specialists usually wish to contribute to the knowledge base of their discipline as well as handing it on to students. Also their education as specialists has usually involved training them as researchers. Retention is affected because trained researchers want to do research. For many staff, a large proportion of academic job satisfaction comes from involvement in knowledge discovery or high level scholarship. Academic research is relevant to quality maintenance because it is a key mechanism by which academic staff train and update themselves.

However, as we showed in chapter 2, the research evidence on the relationship between research and teaching quality is more ambivalent. In particular Hattie and Marsh's (1996) meta-analysis of 58 studies on the relationship between research involvement and lecturer teaching quality convincingly demonstrates that the naturalistic relationship between research and teaching is zero: research excellence is unrelated to teaching quality. While academics that are attracted to lecturing are generally positively motivated towards passing their knowledge on, their skills as researchers do not automatically lead to high quality teaching. Hattie and Marsh wisely conclude that the fact that good teaching is not naturally and intrinsically linked to excellence in research does not mean that a relationship cannot be constructed: 'universities need to set as a mission goal the improvement of the nexus between research and teaching' (Hattie and Marsh, 1996: 533).

There is also research clearly indicating that for many staff their motivation and commitment to academic life is strongly, and in many cases predominantly, concerned with supporting student learning (Boyer, 1990; Ramsden, 1998). Such research also indicates that staff interests and motivations concerning research and teaching may change during a career, and are shaped by perceptions of the reward system. In the particular context of this book, much of the previous research on staff motivations towards teaching and research has to be questioned because teaching and research have been treated as separate categories, and issues such as lecturer motivation to help students understand and do research are generally not effectively captured by such studies. However, the central point is to recognize, as in the earlier discussion in this chapter on student motivation, that in the words of Boyer (1990: 27), faculty are a 'mosaic of talent'; some with particular motivations and skills for research, some for sharing that with students, some for focusing on a pastoral role and so on. The challenge of academic leadership (Ramsden, 1998) is to harness those varied talents, to enable people to grow and change, and to manage the overall department and institution. In this particular context of teaching–research relations, issues of resource management become central.

The resource management issue arises because teaching and research compete for the time, energy and attention of lecturers (Lindsay, 1998). Management of this conflict, evidently the responsibility of government and universities as the agencies responsible for providing and distributing resources in higher education, has been the disaster area of the last decade, certainly from our UK perspective. How has this occurred? This issue takes us into areas of institutional, department and national policies and practices, areas we will consider in detail in chapters 5–7. But in terms of our immediate discussion of lecturer motivation and teaching research links, we consider, particularly but not exclusively from a UK perspective, that central to negative impacts of university management on lecturer motivation are:

- absence of active management;
- poor quality managers;
- inappropriate management strategies;
- inadequate resources for higher education, and a related management culture of control and threats.

The absence of active management has manifested itself at both national and university level by seeking to maximize the output of teaching and research processes as if they were independent systems. In the UK the national mechanisms for judging teaching (the Quality Assurance Agency), and for judging and rewarding research (the Research Assessment Exercise), have operated to deliver carrots and administer sticks, each in studied ignorance and splendid isolation from the other. Within universities an identical self-defeating strategy has been followed, usually by threatening the same academic staff with redundancy if they do not teach more students with diminishing resources and if they do not publish more papers, attract more research funding and take on more consultancy work. At the same time as they exhort academics to produce more research for the benefit of the university, institutions disregard evidence that the result is a weekly workload which breaches the European Union's Working Time Directive (Court, 1996; Wills, 1996), by treating research and teaching as if they were private goods resulting from free individual choice. Wills (1996: 298), in a study revealingly entitled 'Laboring for love? A comment on academics and their hours of work', paints (from research at Southampton University, UK) a daunting picture of academics working long hours, overwork, stress and illness, and that many 'academics felt it was their love of their research and teaching that allowed them to be exploited in this way'.

This unworkable management strategy has at a UK national level resulted from the structural divide between funding systems. At university level it has been pursued because the rapid rise of managerialism in higher education has led to the promotion to management positions of many who lack both management training and competence in strategic thinking. Instead of identifying key problems and showing leadership in establishing priorities and plans, poorly equipped managers have more often resorted to issuing threats, creating insecurity, and seeking to suppress manifestations of discontent. Ramsden's (1998) discussion of these issues suggests that though we have focused on British agencies such as the RAE and QAA, the underlying issues are both general and international.

Factors that impact upon lecturer motivation

Conspicuous features of motivation amongst professional academics in the last decade are that:

- It has become fragmented as the roles of disciplinary specialist, teacher and researcher have become increasingly differentiated and independently assessed and evaluated (Nixon, 1997).

- It has been strained by changes in the student body, in the curriculum, in teaching, in assessment, and in conditions of work (Nixon, 1997; Ramsden, 1998).

- It has been undermined by a fall in income relative to other professions, loss of power and autonomy due to the rise of managerialism, and loss of prestige as university education has become a mass experience instead of an elitist privilege (Ramsden, 1998).

- It has been threatened by the reorganization of universities into units perceived as efficient by managers but which often disregard the tradition of disciplinary cultures.

- It has become confused and distorted by institutional claims to value teaching excellence above all things, while selectively rewarding managerial effort and research success above quality teaching (Gibbs, 1995b; Hattie and Marsh, 1996).

The combined effect of the various factors operating to undermine motivation among university lecturers is an unprecedented loss of morale (Nixon, 1997). Low morale is worsened by the effects of cash starvation resulting from a decade or more of 'efficiency savings'. Financial stringency exerts its maximum effect upon the most vulnerable groups: women, new recruits to the profession and casual staff (Wills, 1996). Individual salary negotiation by researchers attracting heavy funding adds to a general sense of institutional environments as poorly managed, lacking in justice and fairness, and failing to provide rewards commensurate with the length of training required, the commitment in terms of working hours, and the responsibility and stress which lecturers experience (Court, 1996; Wills, 1996). The bleak situation documented particularly well by Wills is extraordinary as an illustration of the perverse way in which universities have failed to use lecturer motivation with respect to research in a rational or strategic manner. Lecturers are almost unique amongst workforces in that they will tolerate relatively low pay and heavy teaching loads to gain access to opportunities to do research. Instead of being content to use research as a motivator in this way, universities have instead increasingly moved towards making research compulsory, emphasizing its function in obtaining university income. The effect of this has been to destroy the value of research as a motivator to individual staff concerns and indeed, to make research activity aversive.

Using research to raise morale and regenerate lecturer motivation

Although the state of morale among lecturing staff in most (UK) universities is alarmingly low, there are a number of grounds for cautious optimism. The imposition of corporate culture on to the university sector has not been a success, but the commitment of lecturers to learner support and knowledge generation has wavered little even as morale has declined. Hopefully a new generation of managers is coming to the fore with an awareness of the mistakes made by their predecessors, a preparedness to tackle ignored but fundamental problems, and a realization that good management does not require a 'managerialist' outlook. Locally, HEFCE is showing signs of recognizing that the RAE is driving universities to draw increasingly heavily upon resources ostensibly available for supporting student learners. The RAE has already assigned stated parity of esteem to pedagogic research, and debates are breaking out about how links between research and teaching can be fostered.

The motivational levers, which can restore faculty morale to a healthy level, are there to be grasped. Recognition of what academics value provides clear indicators to important sources of potential motivational regeneration:

- Academics value the opportunity to participate in research activity.

- Academics value personal interaction with students.

- Academics value professional autonomy.

- Academics value disciplinary culture.

- Academics value participative decision processes.

It is an increasingly essential task for universities actively to address the problems of low morale and diminished motivation which express themselves in terms of fewer students undertaking research training, falling recruitment to the profession, higher incidence of stress and illness, high levels of career dissatisfaction, and increased rates of early retirement (Wills, 1996).

Staff motivational strategies that managers should cultivate include:

- Manage teaching, research, and the interaction between them.

- Encourage identification of links with teaching in research proposals.

- Ensure that high quality researchers teach and/or are involved in course design across all levels.

- Recognize and reward currency of staff knowledge.

- Establish incentives for good teaching.

- Foster consultation and participation.

- Provide opportunities for professional development.

- Promote fairness.

- Eschew inhumane and illegal labour practices.

- Equalise access to research.

- Value all of the many types of research.

IN CONCLUSION

This chapter provides a bridge between the review of the research evidence of teaching-research relations in chapter 2 and the more practical and policy orientated chapters that follow. Claims made within the chapter are themselves firmly grounded in research evidence, and are focused mainly upon student and to a somewhat lesser extent, lecturer motivation, in relation to the teaching–research nexus. In our view, this focus on the research evidence in chapters 2 and 3 gives greater legitimacy and validity to the chapters that follow, and enables us to build on this foundation. We turn first to the level of analysis and action that is under the immediate control of individual staff and course teams, and how courses can be designed by staff to maximize teaching–research linkages, before proceeding to analyse relations at levels where management becomes central, in institutions, departments and national systems. But first let us focus on areas where we have some autonomy and control, the courses we design.

4

Designing the curriculum to link teaching and research

Teaching and research are correlated when they are co-related... .
[One way to achieve this is to] exploit further the link between
teaching and research in the design of courses.
(Brew and Boud, 1995a: 272)

Examples of strategies to increase the relationship between teaching
and research include the following: Increase the skills of staff to teach
emphasizing the construction of knowledge by students rather than
the imparting of knowledge by instructors... develop strategies across
all disciplines that emphasize the uncertainty of the task and
strategies within the disciplines... ensure that students experience the
process of artistic and scientific productivity.
(Hattie and Marsh, 1996: 534)

A constructive developmental view of learning involves two major
concepts: (1) that students construct knowledge by organizing
knowledge and making meaning of their experiences, and (2) that
this construction takes place in the context of their evolving conceptions of knowledge itself and students' role in creating it.
(Baxter Magolda, 1999a: 6)

This chapter sets out principles and provides examples of ways to design
the curriculum in ways that exploit the potential synergies between (staff)
research and student learning. The suggestions are aimed at supporting
the individual academic and also the course team. There are also implications raised here for departmental organization and institutional and
national management and quality assurance that will be developed in
subsequent chapters. While the ideas and suggestions can be developed

and implemented by individuals, they of course have greater impact on student learning when they are progressively developed by course teams and supported by departmental, institutional and national structures.

Our starting points are the ideas and findings of the two previous chapters. In chapter 2 we showed that the nexus between research and student learning was not automatic and had to be created purposefully. In chapter 3 we showed how both student and lecturer motivation could be harnessed to more effectively link teaching and research. In particular there is now a strong body of research on student motivation and learning that indicates how to design curricula and teach in ways that harness student motivation. Also lecturer motivations for research and for teaching can be effectively combined to aid students in learning about and through research.

We do need to emphasize that the ideas and examples presented here are 'work in progress', for there has been little systematic writing on how to design the curriculum explicitly to link teaching and research. As academics we have spent a long time professing and analysing the relationship. We are only just beginning now to propose how to exploit the potential links. Most of the texts on curriculum design ignore this principle. Texts on curriculum design that do in part address linking teaching and research include Stark and Lattuca (1997), who look at how conceptions of disciplinary knowledge shape how the curriculum is designed, and Jenkins (1998), who provides suggestions and case studies of good practice for linking teaching and research in the context of geography. Rowland's (2000) analysis of how staff can approach teaching as a field of passion and inquiry is also relevant to our argument.

In this chapter we purposely do not fully address issues of dissertation, senior thesis courses and research training, for they are well addressed elsewhere, for instance Henry (1995), Ryder and Leach (1997) and McCartney and Brown (1995). For while projects, dissertations and honours theses are critical areas for linking staff research and student learning, our argument is that the linkage needs to be a much more pervasive one. In our experience, when the issue of (undergraduate) students knowing about and doing research are discussed, too often the exclusive focus of the discussion is on the final year dissertation or honours thesis (and the specialist training in research methods that underpin that work). To repeat, we believe these are immensely important and in the discussion of institutional planning we will discuss how these 'capstone' research courses can be provided for all or most students: but our primary focus in this chapter is how the wider curriculum enables students to both understand and do research.

Our hope is that this book may prompt others to build critically on the ideas and strategies we present here, and provide for their colleagues examples from the full range of disciplines. Such disciplinary case studies are important, for as we saw in chapter 2 the form of the relationship may be shaped by the discipline, and it is our experience that many academics move to change their own practice through considering brief practical case studies (from their own discipline). At some point these case studies do need to be set in a conceptual framework, but focused descriptions, such as the one below, provide a useful starting point.

A YEAR ONE ASSIGNMENT

For over ten years the geography department at University College, London (UK) has required all year one students to do an assignment in the first term, in which students interview a member of department academic staff about their research. The assignment has taken two slightly different forms (Dwyer, 2001).

The original model was conceived as part of a compulsory year one course on 'Ideas in Geography'. Staff often see such courses as important in revealing how ideas and research directions in the discipline develop. However, students may fail to connect these more abstract issues to their own understanding of the discipline and to their own concerns and motivations. To aid these connections, the UCL course team required students in tutorial groups of about five to interview a member of staff in the department about the development of his or her research, and his or her views on research directions in the discipline, and then to write an analysis of the interview. After the interviews were completed, a panel symposium of staff helped students see their individual interview as part of the development of ideas in the discipline.

The present model takes the same interview based approach but with the focus on enabling 'students to think about the process of doing research as the first stage in their own research training' (Dwyer, 2001: 359). The students' instructions state 'the aim of this project is to enable you to gain an in-depth understanding of some of the processes and challenges of undertaking geographical research by focusing on the experiences of one member of the geography department at UCL' (Dwyer, 2001: 366). The basic procedures are:

- Each first year tutorial group is allocated a member of staff who is not their tutor.

- Tutorial groups are given by that member of staff three pieces of writing that are representative of their work and their CV and arrange a date for the interview.

- Before the interview students are to read these materials and develop an interview schedule and so on.

- On the basis of their reading and the interview, each student individually writes a 1,500-word report on, first, the objectives of the interviewee's research; second, how the interviewee's research relates to his or her earlier studies; and third, *how the interviewee's research relates to his or her teaching, other interests and geography as a whole* (emphasis added).

CASE STUDY ANALYSED

This brief description provides a clear example, from one department in one discipline, of two linked ways of designing the (first year) curriculum to link teaching and research, and in this case explicitly to link departmental staff research and student learning. In reading it you may question elements of it, and you may consider how you could adapt this idea to address such concerns. For example, does it present the teacher as 'hero' or 'heroine', how does the student (and/or the course) set this particular academic's account in a wider context, and how are the students assisted to appraise critically that context? You may also wonder whether this fits the nature of research in your discipline, particularly in those sciences where much research is done in teams. You may want to adapt the idea to reveal more about consultancy, research based practice, or the nature of research funding, particularly in some disciplines. Requiring that one of the three pieces of writing be a bid for funds to support a research project, an example of paid consultancy or an analysis of professional practice might be an effective way of developing student understanding of how funding and professional practices shape work and research in that discipline. Furthermore, the UCL model operates in a 'research led' institution and a department where all academic staff are centrally involved in research. In other departments, where only some or even no staff are 'high level' researchers, such an exercise may be inappropriate or need considerable modification.

In short, you may question whether such an exercise is appropriate for first year students in your department. The original idea (Cosgrove, 1981) was developed for a final graduating year 'Ideas in Geography' module at the then Oxford Polytechnic, which was then essentially a teaching only institution receiving effectively no funding for research. Here, the exercise concentrated on all full time staff being publicly interviewed on the nature of the ideas that were current in their contrasting undergraduate and postgraduate training and subsequent career, including the courses they currently taught. The course in part aimed at 'helping the graduating student with a perspective on recent changes in (the) discipline' (Cosgrove,

1981: 19). In conclusion Cosgrove (p 22) argued this course offered other departments and disciplines 'possibilities for further elaboration of the basic idea'. UCL was one such department that adapted that original model, and versions of it are now in place at the geography departments of Liverpool John Moores University (see below) and Manchester University, and no doubt elsewhere. Its longevity at UCL, where different staff have decided that it fits their conception of student needs in two contrasting introductory courses, further suggests that it is a model worth considering, and perhaps adapting or using as a stimulus to developing a very different course to meet your students' needs and staff interests.

GOING BEYOND THE DEPARTMENT

The geography BA degree at Liverpool John Moores University (not a research based university) includes a compulsory third year graduating synoptic course on 'Urban and Geographical Thought'. A required essay assignment states 'With regards to a key geographer or urbanist, summarize the main features of her/his work, show how this relates to methodology, and develop critiques of this work from one of the method- ological perspectives presented in the module.' This assignment requires extensive bibliographic work – and being well prepared through the initial stages of the course – and should the scholar still be alive (!) students may contact the researcher by email to ascertain specific questions. (They are not allowed to do a study of staff in their department.)

CASE STUDIES IN PERSPECTIVE

Here it is important to emphasize that these case studies involve only certain and perhaps limited strategies for linking teaching and research. They focus on students' understanding of (staff) research, and not students as active researchers. Their strength lies in part in their clear and imagi- native design; and in the context of this publication making quite concrete the overall perspective of chapter 2 on the research evidence; that the teaching–research nexus has to be created purposefully and tailored to the course, disciplinary and institutional contexts.

These case studies also need to be seen in the context of general prin- ciples of course design; for then they have an added power in shaping how individuals and course teams can develop their own practice. Thus we, and perhaps more critically the UCL department, see that case study as a way of inducting students to learning in a research led department. In chapter 2 we reported on research at Oxford Brookes, which showed that many undergraduate students were unaware of staff research, and the reasons why they carried out research. Even in an institution such as Oxford Brookes, which is not part of the research elite, that is not good 'management' of student expectations and motivations. University College is an institution with a clear focus on international level research, and all departments and individual staff are required to support that institutional commitment. One thing this exercise does is to induct students into learning in an international research led department. Students on entry to the department realize that a central role of staff is to carry on research and that teaching is but one of their responsibilities. Effectively students are being 'managed' to recognize that on certain days and periods staff are not going to be available for them. More positively, students are also starting a process of understanding the role of research in the discipline, the nature of a research led or enriched curriculum, and seeing that they too will be required to carry out research based enquiry. In subsequent courses the geography curriculum at UCL builds on this induction, with many upper level courses being taught by research teams where the curriculum is directly shaped by current research, and culminates with all students carrying out a final year dissertation or thesis. Such an introductory course requirement, and those research based courses that follow on from it, are perhaps also demonstrating the added value that students should get from learning in a research based department, which in many state systems will require them (and /or their parents) to pay extra fees for the privilege.

CONCEPTUAL CURRICULA FRAMEWORKS

While such case studies have evident power in making explicit key ideas in curriculum design, they also need to be set in some wider conceptual framework to enable staff to transfer such practices to their own contexts and to develop a deep understanding of effective course design to link teaching and research. We are also well aware that the power and effectiveness of the UCL case study may also reinforce a view that linking teaching and research focuses on staff telling students about their research; while as we saw in chapter 2 our interpretation of the research evidence shifts some or much of the implications for policy and practice away from staff as researchers towards students as learners. To aid that shift we offer here a provisional model that sets out how teaching and research can be linked from a perspective that focuses on student learning. It is but a model or conceptual framework. It does draw on our reading of the research evidence and our understanding of effective teaching practice. It will shape the discussion that follows in this chapter.

A FRAMEWORK FOR LINKING STUDENT LEARNING AND STAFF RESEARCH: FROM THE PERSPECTIVE OF STUDENT LEARNING

Linking teaching and research is achieved when:

- Students learn how research within their discipline leads to knowledge creation.
- Students are introduced to current research in their disciplines.
- Students learn the methods used to carry out research in their disciplines.
- Students are motivated to learn through knowledge of and direct involvement in research.
- Students carry out research.
- Students participate in research conducted by their lecturers.
- Students learn and are assessed by methods resembling research procedures in their discipline.
- Students learn how research is organized and funded.
- Students become members of a school or department and university culture within which learning, research and scholarship are integrated.
- Students' learning is supported by systems and structures at departmental, institutional, and national level that facilitate staff scholarship and research in the pedagogy of the disciplines as well as disciplinary scholarship and research.

Linking teaching and research is also achieved through:

- University staff at all levels basing practice and policy on knowledge and learning obtained through research (and reflections on practice).
- Academic staff using current pedagogic research findings when designing and delivering courses.
- Institutional managers and national policy makers basing policies – including those on teaching–research relations – on the best available research and scholarly evidence.

SUGGESTED STRATEGIES

Below we set out a range of strategies that we consider useful in identifying general principles for linking teaching and research that can be adapted by individuals and course teams; the rest of the chapter then develops each of these strategies. We have devised these strategies through considering our own and our immediate colleagues' practice; by reading the available literature that provides examples and discussion of these issues. They are also informed by our conceptual model of research and research links from a student learning perspective. We trust readers will build on this suggested schema by revising it, and in particular by building case studies of good practice, such as the UCL case study above, that fit their discipline and institutional context. We also point out that this focus on linking teaching and research is but one way of designing the curriculum.

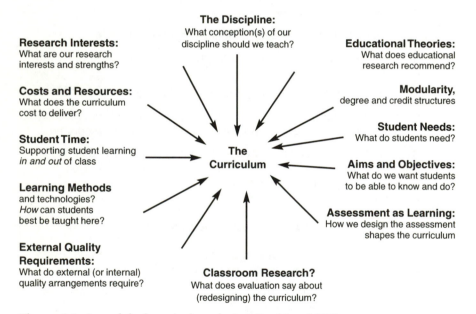

Figure 4.1 A model of curriculum design (Jenkins, 1998)

One of us (Jenkins, 1998) has likened effective curriculum design to staff controlling a Ouija board (Figure 4.1), where the curriculum is seen as a product of a range of forces, including supporting student learning out of class; aims and objectives; changing external quality requirements; theories of student learning; available resources, including staff time; linking teaching and research, and so on. Staff seek to control, shape and prioritize these forces in terms of their and their students' interests. Linking teaching and research is but one of these forces, but it is the one that we are concerned with here, a strategy that can harness staff and students motivations. After presenting the strategies that we think will effectively link teaching and research, we consider each of the principles and go on to provide brief descriptions of curricula from a range of disciplines that demonstrate them in action.

While the overall focus is on linking teaching and research we recognize that the form of that relationship will be shaped by the disciplinary (or interdisciplinary or multidisciplinary) frameworks in which staff and students work; that in certain disciplines research may be closely geared to professional concerns; and that consultancy may be more central to staff responsibilities and to their and their students' motivations. In a context where research is becoming more central to the world of work and employment (Garrick and Rhodes, 2000), we do point to these issues in the model and discussion below, but assume that readers will adapt this overall perspective to the role of research (and consultancy) in their discipline.

STRATEGIES FOR COURSE DESIGN

Strategy 1: develop students' understanding of research

- Develop the curriculum to bring out current /or previous research developments in the discipline.

- Develop student awareness of learning from staff involvement in research (and perhaps research based consultancy and professional practice).

- Develop student understanding of how research is organized and funded in the discipline, institution and profession.

Strategy 2: Develop students' abilities to carry out research

- Students learn in ways that 'mirror' research processes.

- Assess students in ways that mirror research processes.

- Provide training in relevant research skills and knowledge.

- Ensure students experience courses that require them to do research projects, and that there is a progressive move to projects of greater complexity.

- Develop student involvement in staff research.

Strategy 3: Progressively develop students' understanding

- Ensure that introductory courses induct students into the role of research in their discipline and present knowledge as created, uncertain and contested.

- Ensure that advanced courses develop students' understanding of research, and progressively develop their capacities to do research.

- Ensure that graduating year courses require students to carry out a major research study and help them to integrate their understanding of (the role of) research in their discipline or interdisciplines.

Strategy 4: Manage student experience of research

- Limit the negative consequences for students of staff involvement in research and consultancy.

- Evaluate and research student experience of research and consultancy and feed that back into the curriculum.

- Support students in making clear to them the employability elements of research and consultancy.

STRATEGY 1: DEVELOP STUDENTS' UNDERSTANDING OF RESEARCH

In setting out this strategy we are asserting that university education is about inducting and developing students into a view of knowledge as changing through the process of enquiry. Though this principle also should be developed from the earliest years of schooling, at university level it needs to be paramount that we see research and the 'uncertainty' basis of knowledge as its central defining characteristic (see chapter 2). Among the more specific strategies to achieve this aim are the following.

Develop the curriculum to bring out current or previous research

Stark and Lattuca (1997: 244), from a US perspective, comment that 'entering college students often believe that research is a process that occurs primarily in science fields.... In interviewing faculty members teaching introductory courses, we found that they devoted little time to increasing student awareness of research in their field.' A report by the Association of American Colleges (1990, cited in Baxter Magolda, 2000b) concluded that:

the problem is that it [the major] often delivers too much knowledge with too little attention to how that knowledge is being created, what methods and modes of inquiry are employed in its creation, what presuppositions inform it, and what entailments flow from its particular way of knowing.
(Baxter Magolda, 2000b: 12)

Our first year focus group of adult nursing students at Oxford Brookes were initially surprised by their first year course's emphasis on nursing as enquiry, of nursing as a research based profession. On entry to the course, they thought that health care research was carried out by doctors in hospitals; and were surprised to see the course present their future role of a nurse as someone who should understand and use current research in the particular disciplinary professional context of evidence based health care and professional practice. This introductory year one course presented them as someone who might be directly involved in doing research in their degree and later as a professional in practice. While reflecting the disciplinary and in particular the professional concerns of developing graduate health professionals who could undertake evidence based practice, the aim of the course was in effect to challenge such false preconceptions of the role and value of research in their course and subsequent professional practice. The first year course at UCL, and the graduating course from the then Oxford Polytechnic, clearly direct students to see the role of research in shaping and reshaping the changing and contested nature of knowledge. To repeat, we consider that this view of knowledge as being created, uncertain and contested should be central to all university curricula, whether staff are research active or are not themselves (centrally) involved in discovery research. In discussing this principle we have purposefully focused on stage or year one courses. Clearly we believe this principle should pervade the curriculum and be developed in upper level courses. Often they can more readily link to staff research interests. This principle will reflect disciplinary concerns and will be discussed in chapter 7, when we consider the role of disciplinary associations.

Develop student awareness of learning from staff involvement in research

Clearly this principle is most, and perhaps solely, appropriate to those departments and institutions where staff are active in discovery research (and in research based consultancy or professional practice). However it can be developed to recognize that some staff and some departments may concentrate on more scholarly activities, and such staff activities are formally linked to the curriculum. It could also be developed, for example, through video conference links with research active staff in other institutions, while in certain disciplines or HE institutions, involving researchers in regional industries and or professional organizations may be a more appropriate way of developing student understanding of research in the discipline.

Develop student understanding of how research and consultancy is organized and funded in the discipline, institution and profession

The form that research takes in the discipline should clearly shape the particular curricula that are devised. Relevant factors include the extent to which research is individual or team based, how it is funded and organized, and the extent to which it is focused on improving practice through consultancy. It may also be important that this understanding of research should include questioning of aspects of that research; for example ensuring the curriculum addresses issues of the ethics of funding, of gender, ethnicity, national or corporate dominance and control of the organization and the nature of the research. The extent to which these more sociological concerns of research organization are developed in the curriculum will clearly vary by discipline and individual and course team staff interests.

STRATEGY 2: DEVELOP STUDENTS' ABILITIES TO CARRY OUT RESEARCH

For all university curricula there is a pressing need to present the world as a place of uncertainty and of the role of research in both opening up that uncertainty and helping ourselves as individuals and society at large to understand and manage it. This perspective, a world of 'super-complexity', and the curricula implications for universities it should require, have been powerfully argued by Barnett, indicated in chapter 2. In drawing attention to the postmodern questioning of the certainty of knowledge and the complexity of the changes in the worlds in which students live, and will live through, Barnett argues:

> Unfortunately, lecturers too often possess a concept of teaching that places students in a subservient position such that they are the recipients of a curriculum instead of largely making it themselves. The issue, then, is whether the conditions of super complexity will prompt the lecturers to adopt teaching approaches that are likely to mirror the lecturers' experience as researchers.
> (Barnett, 2000: 163)

An understanding of the nature of research in the discipline can develop students' understanding of complexity. However as Barnett suggests (ibid), the key to this process is to design a curriculum that enables students to mirror the lecturers' experience as researchers, to develop students' abilities to carry out research in their discipline.

Central to this process, as Barnett himself argues, is a focus on how students learn and are assessed. As we argued in chapter 2, there are elements of Boyer's (1990) critique of the dominance of the discovery research culture that direct attention to strengthening the linkage between (staff) research and how students learn. In the context of a high prestige research university, a Boyer Commission study (backed by the Carnegie Foundation) that looked at ways of implementing Boyer's ideas argued that:

> The experience of most undergraduates at most research universities is of receiving that which is served out to them. In one course after another they listen, transcribe, absorb and repeat.... The ideal embodied in this report would turn the prevailing undergraduate culture of receivers into a culture of enquiry, a culture in which faculty, graduate students and undergraduates share a culture of enquiry.
> (Boyer Commission, University of Stony Brook, 1998)

In the United States much of this reform movement has in part focused on science curricula, too many of which are seen as embodying the principles of subservience and repetition, but also 'the curriculum is often designed to identify and encourage the relatively few students who wish to be researchers themselves' (Rameley, 1997: 130).

In the United States and Canada there has been a strong push to make such inquiry and research based courses an integral part of the overall year one curriculum for all students. To anticipate chapter 5, many institutions have guaranteed all first year students at least one course which is taught by experienced staff in an enquiry format, with assessment that is either essay or project based. Often such courses are in effect based around staff (developing) research interests and are in effect collaborative student and staff research projects. While many of the strongest examples of such courses are at the small rich private teaching-focused institutions, the principle has also been adapted at public state universities.

More specific ways in which students can develop the abilities to carry out research include the following.

Students learn in ways that mirror research processes

The US reform movement in college science teaching charted this principle well by arguing for learning science 'by direct experience with the methods and processes of inquiry' (National Research Council, 1996, cited in McNeal and D'Avanzo, 1997: V). Such curricula for all students, whether they are science majors or not, whether they are seeking a science based career or not, mirror the research processes in scientific research and support student understanding of and ability to do research. Such learning (taken from McNeal and D'Avanzo, 1997: V1):

● is investigative;

● is often collaborative;

● comes from working on complex, often real world problems;

● engages students in interpreting data and where possible, in gathering their own data;

● shows students the limitations as well as the powers of particular scientific ways of knowing.

Baxter Magolda (1999a) contributes two ethnographic studies of courses at Miami, Ohio (USA) which illustrate these general principles well. An advanced course in 'Winter Biology' focused on helping 'students think like scientists: learn how to explore the scientific literature, identify useful questions, understand how to determine the next step in a research effort, and learn the communication skills to function in a scientific community... and understand how the knowledge creation effort in the discipline took place' (p 103). The first part of this course involved the lecturers modelling these processes with reference to their research and that of others: the second part centred on students writing a research paper, presenting it at a scientific conference, and then writing a grant proposal based on the research paper. A course on 'Mathematics by Inquiry' sought to 'help students understand that mathematical ideas and rules were created by humans and that they, as humans, could participate in the creation process' (p 137). Central to the course were the methods of teaching and inquiry, which were active and collaborative, with students working in groups and with the instructor. The course was structured so that the initial focus was on students and staff focusing on *discovering* the structure of mathematics, then moving to *synthesis* of their understanding of that information and structure, and then concluding with an emphasis on *applying* maths structure in practice.

Clearly the way this principle is developed must recognize how research is conducted in that discipline, suitably modified to meet the particular student group. Thus, in certain professional disciplines such as planning, hotel management and so on, learning about research and consultancy is likely to emphasize pedagogic methods such as case studies, problem solving, and projects which involve or simulate project costing and project planning.

Assess students in ways that mirror research processes

Given the critical role we know that assessment plays in shaping how students approach their studies, this means we need to align the methods of assessment and the assessment tasks to our overall goals of getting students to be research aware and skilled. There has been little explicit attention in the literature as to how to achieve this, but some provisional suggestions include:

- Make the task one that has students simulate writing an article for a learned journal (and using the effective assessment criteria for that journal), or writing a consultancy report.

- Make the task one where students (perhaps in groups) make a bid proposal to carry out a research project. Here the assessed task is likely to emphasize the research design and project plan.

- Ensure the assessment criteria support developing student understanding of research and knowledge of research methods.

- As academics we generally show our work to others, and then revise it before submitting it to a journal or research granting authority. So students can be required to have their work reviewed by others in the class. These student reviewers are then trained in how to referee and review research articles, with particular attention to research based assessment criteria such as the appropriateness of the research methodology. The final version might include a commentary by the student on how he or she had taken into account (or decided to reject) the views of his or her peers.

- Have students present their work at a simulated research conference (possibly with external observers and assessors, for instance, researchers from another institution or professional body).

- Have students present their work for assessment as contributions to a journal or edited collection on a topic. Web based publishing allows this to be done both cheaply and publicly: and enables students (and staff) to get feedback on their research from researchers worldwide. (This is further developed in chapter 5 on institutional strategies.)

INTRODUCTION TO RESEARCH METHODS FOR HEALTH PROFESSIONALS

The radiography and physiotherapy undergraduate degree at Keele University (UK) includes in year one a psychology based research methods course.

> Students were given... a hypothetical problem relevant to their profession... and then, working in teams of six to eight students, they carried out a survey of members of the general public. Each team had to produce a report on their research according to the author guidelines for a key journal in their profession that could be submitted for publication. Teams then exchanged reports and each student acted as referee for the journal and produced an evaluation report. This 'referees report' was submitted as assessed written work for the module.
> (Hegarty, 1998, 162)

STUDENTS' TEAMS FROM YEARS 1–3 AT SUNDERLAND UNIVERSITY AND THE CITY COUNCIL

Part of the core spine of the environmental studies degree at the University of Sunderland (UK) 'are integrative environmental issues modules at each level. The second semester delivery of these modules brings together first, second and third year students for a local sustainability project. The students work in mixed level small research groups looking at various aspects of sustainable development in collaboration with Sunderland City Council. In 2000 each group was set the academic task of producing a sustainability profile for one of Sunderland's wards. There was a differentiation of roles and learning outcomes between levels:

- Level three students were directed to take a lead in the project management.

- Level two students in data analysis and shaping data collection strategies.

- Level one students in fieldwork and basic research.

Each student team was required to submit a 5,000 word joint report on their particular ward and to present their findings at a public conference attended by city councillors, external partners and invited members of their local communities.'
(Hughes *et al*, 2001: 5–6)

Provide training in relevant research skills and knowledge

Certainly in the UK most courses in the sciences and social sciences provide direct training in research methods. These generally begin in a limited way in year one and are then progressively developed in subsequent courses, culminating in the honours thesis or dissertation. These are clearly central to developing students' ability to do research. To repeat, we do see such courses as central to developing an effective teaching–research nexus, but because they are well developed in both practice and in other available texts, the issue is not further developed here.

Develop student involvement in staff research

Explicitly involving students in staff led research can clearly support staff in seeing their teaching and their research as being co-related, with clear potential gains for both staff and students. In particular students can gain understanding, in a relatively safe or controlled environment, of the organization and funding of research, research design, and of course the actual subjects of investigation. Such involvement can range from using the results of the raw data from staff research projects to full involvement in the research itself. It is a model that clearly fits the way research is often organized in the sciences where a lot of research is done in teams, often with clear leaders where an overall project can be subdivided so that individuals or small groups of students can take on relatively discrete investigations. In a particular course or project students may only do one or two aspects of the research process, such as problem formulations and research design, but by placing those aspects in the overall research design, staff can ensure students develop understanding of the complete process. For example, the geology department at the Canberra College of Advanced Education developed a long term student and staff research project to map areas of New South Wales for the State Geological Survey (McQueen *et al*, 1990). Such a science-based model can be adapted to other disciplinary contexts. In the institutional context of the University of Michigan's service learning 'Arts of Citizenship program', humanities staff working with community groups have involved (and assessed!) students in a range of long term research projects (http://www.artsofcitizenship.umich.edu/). The overall course named 'Community Projects in the Humanities' has four to five long term mega projects, and each of these has 15–16 strands, for instance dance forms in inner city communities in Baltimore in the 1940s and 1950s, within which students can develop a research project that is limited in both duration and timing (Scobey, 2002). Students here see their research project as part of a bigger whole and also as contributing to published work and local community activities and needs.

Clearly there are both limitations and dangers to this strategy. Limitations include the limited role students are likely to play in the research design; dangers include students perceiving themselves as unpaid research assistants and the curriculum as distorted mainly to meet staff needs and interests. But potentially this strategy can meet both student and staff needs (Krochalk and Hope, 1995). The case study in the box is a well documented example of this and related strategies.

SOCIAL ADMINISTRATION RESEARCH PROJECT

Social policy students in the University of Brighton social and administration degree did a second year project that staff commissioned from a sponsoring social policy agency, for example, patient satisfaction with an accident and emergency department, commissioned and funded by a Regional Health Authority (Winn, 1995). Stanier (1995) provides a related account of geography students working with a Family Health Service Authority. Although the course is no longer taught 'as student numbers increased and students increasingly took part time employment, restricting their ability to do the fieldwork' (Winn, 2001), the central features of the Brighton course were:

- In years one and two, students undertook compulsory research methods courses, which progressively developed students' ability to do research.

- 'The other major component of the second year programme is participation in the commissioned research project… [one of the central aims of which is] to give students insights relating to the commissioning, funding, planning and management of research projects' (Winn, 1995: 207). While some of these students may graduate to research positions, the majority, will 'become practitioners or policy makers, careers in which they may not be directly involved in research, but where the ability to understand and evaluate the research of others, and perhaps to commission or supervise research are essential skills' (p 204). This project based course was designed to address such issues as the political and policy context of much research, and students' future employment and roles. It was also designed, through its 'real world' practical character, to motivate social science students for whom such courses are generally compulsory; but many of whom 'have a longstanding aversion to quantitative and technical aspects of the subject' (p 204).

- Prior to the six-month course staff had agreed with the Authority issues of access, overall research design and costing. 'The project was costed to cover university staff time additional to that which would be required to run a research methods course which did not involve a research project, staff and student expenses, and materials. Students' time was not

included in the costing, and the research was organized so that participation in the project did not make demands on students' time beyond
those normally required by the syllabus' (p 207).

- Winn (p 211) concludes that 'perhaps the greatest potential gains from
  this type of project is that it allows students to develop an understanding
  of the process of doing research by following a research project from its
  early stages to a conclusion.'

STRATEGY 3: PROGRESSIVELY DEVELOP STUDENTS' UNDERSTANDING

- Ensure that introductory courses induct students into the role of research in their discipline and present knowledge as uncertain and contested.

- Ensure that advanced courses develop students' understanding of research, and progressively develop their capacities to do research.

- Ensure that graduating year courses require students to carry out a major research study and help them to integrate their understanding of the role of research in their discipline (or interdisciplines).

In the introduction to this chapter we focused on the case study of the introductory interview exercise at University College London, and portrayed
that as an example of the general principle of inducting students into the
culture and curriculum of that particular course team. We also indicated
that the assignment was only an introduction. Its strength, in part, lay in
the way that the whole course progressively developed the culture of a
research led curriculum, through specialist team-taught upper level
courses around staff research themes, and a course structure that required
students to do research projects at growing levels of complexity and inde-
pendence. To repeat an earlier theme from the introduction to this chapter,
while the ideas discussed here can be developed by individuals and small
groups of staff, they will have a much greater impact on student learning
when they are developed across the whole course team. The sociology case
study in the box illustrates this critical principle.

RESEARCH-LED TEACHING IN SOCIOLOGY AT BIRMINGHAM

Birmingham University (UK) in its 'Learning and Teaching Strategy' describes itself as a 'research led institution... [providing] a research centred environment in which students undertake and reflect on their studies' (University of Birmingham, 2000: 1). The sociology undergraduate programme expresses this in several ways. In particular the course team has designed a structured programme to progressively develop students as researchers and their knowledge of research.

- Active researchers teach students, and particularly in the third graduating year specialist options strongly reflect staff research interests.

- There is a commitment to ensure that students themselves engage with research from the outset of their programme. In the first year compulsory course, 'Introduction to Sociology', the first assessment requires students to conduct some rudimentary research on an urban environment. This is to inculcate the view that research constructs knowledge, as well as to develop students' abilities to undertake research.

- This curriculum focus on urban issues clearly reflects department research interests in the reinvention of Birmingham as a city, and this is clearly developed in the lectures and reading for this introductory module.

- In this first year assignment students are free to do research on any city or town. The issues they research are very variable, for example, inequality and deprivation in the city; the growth of services; the decline of manufacture; post-modernity and the city; youth in the city, and so on. Students need to decide how best to investigate their problem, but will be required to learn about gathering statistics on a locality, contacting key decision-makers and identifying subjects for interview etc.

- Alongside this module they are also taught compulsory all-year research methods courses which feed technical and ethical awareness into their work.

- In year 2 they are required to produce an assessed research proposal for their year three dissertation. This is part of a compulsory year-long course on 'Questioning Modernity: Sociological Theory and Analysis', which develops their understanding of sociological theories and research methodologies and issues.

- The culmination of their degree is the dissertation which represents 30 per cent of the final degree grade. The dissertation is an independent investigation, and generally involves the student obtaining and analysing original data. This thesis, which is some 10,000 words in length, provides a culmination of the degree, and ensures that the skills and knowledge required to achieve this have been progressively developed through the course. This research emphasis is explained to students as equipping them 'for research in employment or future academic studies' (Webster, 2001).

STRATEGY 4: MANAGE STUDENT EXPERIENCE OF RESEARCH

Aspects of these strategies can be seen in part as a way of 'repackaging' the active pedagogy that is (rightfully) favoured by educational developers in organizations such as SEDA. By contrast, developing strategies to manage student experience of (staff) research takes us into areas which most texts and discussions on curriculum design ignore, yet which are central to the (hidden) curriculum that both staff and students experience. Thus an audit of research–teaching links at Canterbury, Christchurch, New Zealand, commented that:

> In the Forestry report they admitted they are bad at exposing their students to staff research.... The department has pledged to remedy this... since they recognize that an unfortunate consequence is that few of their best students are motivated to research and do not want to undertake postgraduate research.
> (Spronken-Smith *et al*, 2000: 23–4)

So the effective hidden curriculum either did not involve or inform students about staff research and is in effect a case study of 'ineffectively' managing that research. Ways of effectively managing staff research include the following.

Limit negative consequences

When we present findings and conclusions from the Brookes research at conferences there are often strong nods of recognition that students (undergraduates and postgraduates) are frustrated by staff absences or unavailability because of research requirements. There is similar recognition that students are often unaware of, and do not feel that they are stakeholders in, staff research. This recognition is the case in both high ranking research departments and in those that are effectively teaching focused. It is a 'hidden' (Snyder, 1971) or perhaps an 'unmanaged curriculum'. Strategies for minimizing the negative consequences of staff research include:

- Strategies outlined above, for example the case study at UCL, that get students aware of the role of research in the discipline, and involved in staff-led research projects.

- Strategies and exercises such as the UCL case (but adapted to each department and its curriculum) that enable students to understand why staff are involved in research and see it as important in itself, as well as for their own professional career advancement. Students who are aware that (some) staff see their promotion and career advancement as dependent on research performance may question that emphasis, but are in a better position to understand staff perceptions and actions. A central theme of the Brookes focus group research was that few students realized the motivations and career concerns of staff.

- Strategies that give students advanced notice of staff research absences and publicize to students selected results from that research.

- Strategies that minimize the negative consequences of staff absences, be it the use of email or video conferencing to support those students who require specialist expertise, or the deployment of other staff to cover for absence, particularly at key periods when that support is most needed. Such periods certainly include the few weeks before students have to hand in their dissertation or honours thesis. In the UK this is often just after the Easter break, a time when staff may want to be on holiday or doing research! So there are real conflicts that have to be recognized and managed.

- Discussions with students (representatives) may give other useful strategies.

In short, students and staff need to be treated as the adults that they are. The problems need to be recognized and staff (and student) involvement sought in developing strategies to solve or minimize them.

Evaluate and research student experience

Most staff now regularly evaluate aspects of the curriculum, yet in our experience few course teams evaluate whether or how (staff) research is developed and managed through the formal, and the informal or 'hidden' curriculum. Yet if we see the teaching–research linkage as important then it needs to be central to how and what we evaluate. We must then ensure that evaluation is fed into future practice. At Louisiana State University there was a radical redesign of a required science course for non-science majors along 'science as a process of enquiry' principles. A specially designed questionnaire was developed to test whether 'student reaction to an investigative approach would be more positive than to the traditional cook bookish laboratory course and that this would translate into more positive student attitudes to science' (Sundberg, 1997: 150). The Brookes focus group investigations and University of East Anglia student based research study (Zamorski, 2000) represent examples of how a whole institution can look at the student experience of staff research to consider whether students are perceiving benefits from that research. Evidently such evaluations can focus at the level of the individual module up to the level of the whole institution. These institution or department wide investigations can be an initial part of an institutional or departmental change strategy: see chapters 5 and 6.

Support student employability

For many staff their own involvement in research and to an extent their wish to ensure that students benefit from learning in a research environment will be based largely on academic values, and the view that this is the proper role of universities. We have those values and wish our students to share them. However, for many students their motivation (see chapter 3) to gain from the research elements of the curriculum will no doubt be increased by effectively demonstrating to them that the knowledge and skills gained through research will aid their employability. The ways this can be achieved will certainly reflect very different disciplinary practices, and cover how research developed through that discipline can be 'transferred' to potential employers.

Such strategies may well include:

- Ensuring the case studies of research that students learn through the curriculum include elements which demonstrate the importance of that discipline based research to the worlds of work.

- Assessments and activities that support students in translating what they have learnt through research and training and so on, into what employers might value. (Here the support and testimonies of former graduates from the department may assist.)

- Staff assisting students in making their case to potential employees by providing short descriptions of what a graduate should be able to do through the research elements of their degree. This may be particularly important to those disciplines such as the humanities where employers may not readily appreciate how a research training in, say, history may transfer into the worlds of work.

An example of this curriculum principle is that Stockton College (a liberal arts college in New Jersey, USA), as part of its institution wide focus on mathematical reasoning, has this objective for all curricula: 'Students should understand the ways in which *quantitative reasoning serves as an important tool in a variety of disciplines and careers*, and so understand the wide variety of mathematical applications which they may be called upon to understand and use' (Byrne, 1997: 72; emphasis added).

IN CONCLUSION

As we noted earlier in this chapter, how to explicitly link teaching and research in the curriculum has been little discussed in formal (generic) higher education literature. So this chapter is a very provisional structuring of strategies. Below is an alternative but complementary way of conceptualizing how to develop the curriculum to foster teaching–research links. However we conceptualize these linkages, this chapter has shown there is much that individual staff and course teams can do to foster the nexus. However, these linkages will be more effective and pervasive when supported by the institutions, the departments and the national systems, the themes of the next three chapters.

Perspectives from Canterbury

In its submission to the New Zealand's Academic Audit Unit's review of teaching–research links (see chapter 7), the University of Canterbury at Christchurch (2000a: 47) conceived that:

> research and teaching may interrelate through:
>
> *Transmission links*
> Teaching is seen as a means of transmitting new research knowledge (research–teaching link), and involvement in teaching informs and enriches the research process (teaching–research link).
>
> *The process link*
> This teaching model encourages students to engage in a research and critical inquiry approach to learning.
>
> *The research culture link*
> Teachers and students work together in a community of inquiry, and learning provides the vital link between research and teaching.

5

Organizing the institution to link teaching and research

In view of the central nature of research and teaching in HE, and the almost universal assumption that R benefits T, and the importance of scholarship, it is perhaps surprising how relatively few institutions have specific policies in place to either monitor, or to develop and maximise these beneficial synergies.
(JM Consulting, 2000: 16)

The analyses reveal ways in which it is possible to work to strengthen the connections between teaching and research, and highlight that it is valid and important for universities to address the nexus through measures consistent with their mission, goals and objectives. Since universities differ, it is appropriate that the means also differ.
(Zubrick, Reid and Rossiter, 2001: 83)

How does the institution ensure that teaching and learning are different from what would occur if there were no research and how is this difference measured?
(University of Auckland, 2000: 19)

The re-emphasis of undergraduate education is probably the most pressing issue that universities must face in the next decade. The challenge is to demonstrate that the learning and research environments, at the undergraduate level are not competitive but complementary.
(Piper, 2001)

INTRODUCTION

Institutions differ greatly in their histories and cultures, resources, balance between undergraduate and postgraduate education, degree of research activity and income and so on. So any discussion of how institutions can foster a teaching–research nexus must start from a recognition of institutional diversity, and as we show later in this chapter part of that difference may well be how they conceive and deliver the nexus. We also have to recognize that we have very limited research and scholarship to guide us on this issue, certainly in comparison to the vast research literature focusing on the nexus at the level of individual academics (chapter 2). Yet clearly institutions set contexts, policies and allocate resources that shape staff (and student) behaviour. For Clark (1993a), the role of the institution in shaping teaching–research relations is formative, that is, setting a general context, with key *enactment* being at the department level.

We consider that the relative roles of departments and institutions may well vary depending on institution and national system. Perhaps Clark's views reflect the view of the departments in large US research universities. In other state systems and outside the research elite the institution may be a more critical formative and enacting agent.

However, we suspect that in many national systems, including the research elite US universities, the institution is an increasingly important shaper of teaching–research relations. A key factor here is the increasing national, even international, competition that is in part driving institutions to attempt to differentiate themselves and set in place institutional strategies to attempt institutional definition. This institutional focus is certainly the case in the UK where institutions are now required by the Funding Council to have research and teaching strategies. Indeed, funding for teaching is top sliced to ensure and support the development of teaching strategies, many of which profess a commitment to linking teaching and research (see chapter 7). But such moves to devise institutional policies to link teaching and research are an international phenomenon, and are often driven by institutional imperatives, with or without national policy support. Thus the President of University of British Columbia, speaking at a policy retreat with University Governors, stated:

> The re-emphasis of undergraduate education is probably the most pressing issue that universities must face in the next decade.... The challenge is to demonstrate that the learning and research environments, at the undergraduate level are not competitive but complementary.
> (Piper: 2001)

In considering the balance and relation between institutional and department strategies for strengthening the teaching–research nexus we recognize that while departments are often where (linked) disciplinary allegiances are strong, and where policies which build on these values and practices should be based, other strategies such as requirements for graduation, how courses and staff are reviewed and appraised, and how the timetable and curriculum are structured, are often institution based.

So this chapter argues for the central role of institutions in shaping teaching and research relations, and also recognizes that the emphases and the policy levers will vary greatly between and indeed within institutions. While we profess a general view of the importance of institutional planning, we offer a set of strategies and suggest you prioritize, adapt and add to them to fit your particular context. We provide a number of case studies of these strategies which can be adapted by institutions and by departments. The strategies we discuss are set out below.

INSTITUTIONAL STRATEGIES TO LINK TEACHING AND RESEARCH

Developing institutional awareness and institutional mission

- Strategy 1: State that linking teaching and research is central to the institutional mission and formulate strategies and plans to support the nexus.

- Strategy 2: Make it the mission and deliver it.

- Strategy 3: Organize events, research studies and publications to raise institutional awareness.

- Strategy 4: (Use the Boyer/Carnegie analysis to) develop institutional conceptions and strategies to effect teaching–research links.

Developing pedagogy and curricula to support the nexus

- Strategy 5: Develop and audit teaching policies, and implement strategies to strengthen the teaching–research nexus.

- Strategy 6: Use strategic and operational planning and institutional audit to strengthen the nexus.

- Strategy 7: Develop curriculum requirements.

- Strategy 8: Review the timetable.

- Strategy 9: Develop special programmes and structures.

Developing research to support the nexus

- Strategy 10: Develop and audit research policies, and implement strategies to strengthen the teaching–research nexus.

- Strategy 11: Ensure links between research centres, staff scholarship, the curriculum and student learning.

Developing staff and university structures to support the nexus

- Strategy 12: Ensure the nexus is central to policies on inducting and developing new staff, and for strategies to support the professional development of established staff.

- Strategy 13: Ensure teaching–research links are central to policies on promotion and reward.

- Strategy 14: Ensure effective synergies between units, committees and structures for teaching and research.

- Strategy 15: Link with related university strategies.

- Strategy 16: Participate in national programmes.

- Strategy 17: Support implementation at school and department level.

STRATEGY 1: LINKING TEACHING AND RESEARCH AS CENTRAL TO THE INSTITUTIONAL MISSION

Mission statements now abound and we are well aware that they can be formulaic and a poor import from the world of marketing. Yet at best they can help institutions develop a sense of shared purpose, and shape internal and external planning and accountability. For those of us who wish to strengthen teaching–research connections, statements such as this from Southampton University's (2000: 1) 'Learning and Teaching Strategy' can be one element of an effective strategy. 'The University will continue to offer a curriculum which communicates the findings of recent research. The commitment is to an ethos of curiosity-driven inquiry and intellectual excitement on the part of students and staff.'

However, such fine words need to be implemented through a range of strategies, otherwise the reality will be that revealed by the Audit of Exeter University that 'there was very little systematic reflection within the University about just what was meant by the claimed interdependence of research and teaching' (HEQC, 1997: 3). Indeed recent research by Gibbs (2001: 5) on the institutional learning and teaching strategies now required by the English Funding Council (HEFCE) showed that:

> The teaching research nexus was addressed only to a limited extent. It was very rare for institutions to make any mention of their research strategy in their learning and teaching strategy, and the potential conflicts or synergies between research and teaching strategies were generally not addressed.... *Mechanisms through which this nexus might be exploited are not yet articulated.... Strengthening the nexus is at present an aspiration rather than a plan.*
> (HEQC, 1997: 17; emphasis added)

STRATEGY 2: MAKE IT THE MISSION AND DELIVER IT

Most institutions in effect attempt to deliver a range of semi-related strategies, or as one US quip has it, 'a university faculty is united by a common central heating system and grievances over parking'. Realistically linking teaching and research will be one of a range of strategies, and the rest of this chapter suggests ways of delivering that goal in the context of institutions pursuing diverse missions.

However there are a few examples where student based research-enquiry and the linking of teaching and research are right at the centre both in mission and delivery. These include the inquiry based curriculum at Hampshire College (USA) and the project based curriculum at the University of Roskilde, Denmark: see the case studies below.

HAMPSHIRE COLLEGE (AMHERST, MASSACHUSETTS, USA) HTTP://WWW.HAMPSHIRE.EDU/

Hampshire is a small private liberal arts and science institution that has a whole institution focus on inquiry learning (Weaver, 1989; McNeal and D'Avanzo, 1997; Prince and Kelly, 1997). Formed in 1970, the institution sought to develop an 'academic programme... distinctive in its ends as in its means... [with its academic programme focused on] conceptual inquiry... theoretical constructs, propositions, and methodological principles in active inquiry' (Patterson and Longsworth: X11 and X1V, cited in Weaver, 1989: 5).

> What drives and vitalizes the Hampshire system is the commitment to a research-based curriculum – a belief that knowledge is continually being developed and that students, as well as faculty, can actively contribute to knowledge.... Reversing the usual curriculum by beginning with real

questions and problems, is the central element in promoting the skills of critical enquiry and developing student motivation.
(McNeal, 2000)

In a curriculum that is both interdisciplinary and disciplinary the current curricula elements that address the teaching–research nexus include the following.

Beginning/division 1 requirements (approximately year one)
'Students must formulate substantive questions on a range of specific subjects and then reflect critically on the implications of the analytical frameworks and methods they used in pursuing the questions' (Prince and Kelly, 1997: 7).

Division 2 requirements (approximately year two and three)
'Working with at least two or three faculty, students... define a substantive area of study and then specify key questions that will serve as general guides through the concentration (structurally equivalent to majors). In the second step... the student designs a program of study, including courses, fieldwork, internships and independent study' (Prince and Kelly, 1997: 8).

Division 3/Capstone requirements (approximately graduating year)
This is 'primarily devoted to a... thesis or artistic project that culminates with an oral examination' (Prince and Kelly, 1997: 9).

PROJECT-BASED LEARNING AT ROSKILDE
HTTP://WWW.RUC.DK/

The University of Roskilde (Denmark) is one of those HE institutions like Alverno, Evergreen and Hampshire Colleges in the United States that have developed a whole institution approach to pedagogy. In Roskilde's case, this institutional focus is based around students working in groups on student-initiated projects. Roskilde opened in 1972 and its origins are in the radical university politics of the 1960s and Marxist concerns for praxis, that is, integrating theory and practice. It also sees its origins and current policies in the European or Humboldt tradition of the university as an institution that links teaching and research, and is critical that:

> Research has become more specialized and requires more resources. The case is that in most cases research has been transferred to other institutions (i.e. outside universities).... We are inclined to view the university teacher as a teacher who also researches, not a specialized, elite researcher who also teaches.
> (Olesen and Jensen, 1999: 21)

While Roskilde's curricular concerns go far beyond forging teaching–research links, elements of Roskilde (Olesen and Jensen, 1999; Legge, 1997) that represent a whole institution approach to the nexus include:

- In years 1–2 at least 50 per cent of student time for the assessed curriculum is taught through project work.

- The projects involve students working in groups guided by staff. '*Problem-orientated* project work... *are participant* directed indicating that it is the group members that collectively... take the responsibility for the project.... The result is a body of knowledge owned for the most part by the students that produced it and not borrowed from the teachers who taught it' (Legge, 1997: 5; emphasis in original).

- Alongside these project based courses, in years 1 and 2 are more formal courses organized initially in interdisciplinary areas of sciences, humanities and social sciences.

- Advanced courses, which are more linked to formal 'discrete' disciplines such as physics and so on, maintain this project focus and often involve students and staff working together on research projects.

- A distinct feature of Roskilde is that much of the formal and informal learning is in houses, which are discipline based (for example, geography). The rooms at the edge of the house are for staff offices, group project work, and secretarial and computer support for project teams. The centre of the house is a large open plan room where students and staff periodically meet to progress the various projects.

- The traditional university physical layout of lecture theatres and so on is replaced here by a very different architecture and departmental organization to support a radically different pedagogy. This further demonstrates that moving a whole institution to an inquiry based or research-based curriculum must consider many aspects of institutional planning and policy.

In its short institutional history this approach has been, and is, questioned from outside and inside Roskilde. To anticipate the next chapter, one external threat is the external funding for research that often prioritises high-level specialized research which does not easily mesh with this curriculum.

Clearly both Hampshire and Roskilde are very particular institutions bound around one or two key central educational principles and ways of developing the teaching–research nexus. We must now consider the broader range of institutions with more diverse missions. But there are lessons in adapting the principles and strategies from these particular focused institutions to their more diverse institutional missions. In particular, if the nexus is desired then it requires coherent and long term effort developing and using a range of strategies.

STRATEGY 3: ORGANIZE EVENTS, RESEARCH STUDIES AND PUBLICATIONS TO RAISE INSTITUTIONAL AWARENESS

It is clear from reports such as the Audit of Exeter University (QAA, 1997) that many staff (including senior managers) may lack an awareness of the scholarship and research on the nexus, and lack a 'language' to discuss and act on the issues. Depending upon the level of awareness and the urgency of the issues, it may be appropriate to organize events, produce internal publications and Web sites, and carry out action research studies to raise awareness and promote an informed discussion across an institution. This can then lead to or support the formulation of policies and implementation strategies.

This can also celebrate and publicize what is already in place. For example, at Southampton Institute (UK), a new Principal initiated an institution-wide conference, where national and external speakers set out the context of national policies and the research evidence, and internal speakers discussed dilemmas and possible strategies for the Institute (Southampton Institute, 1998). Oxford Brookes University (UK) ran a similar event, but added a Web site where staff were encouraged to put examples of good practice of curricula, which linked teaching and research: http://www.brookes.ac.uk/services/ocsd/5_research/link1/ltr1.html.

The University of Sydney, in the context of a university project led by Paul Ramsden, the Pro Vice Chancellor (Learning and Teaching), to 'enhance students' learning experiences by progressing the ways in which undergraduate teaching is informed by research' (Brew, 2001b: 3), organized an institutional 'Showcase of Scholarly Inquiry in Teaching and Learning', which, while including external speakers, mainly featured university staff presenting on five themes, including the use of disciplinary research in teaching, engaging students in inquiry in teaching and discussions on bringing research and teaching together (http://www.itl.usyd.edu.au/itl/docs/search/default.htm).

SYMPOSIUM AND IMPLEMENTATION AT MASSEY UNIVERSITY

In advance of a national three yearly audit which in 2000–01 focused on teaching–research relations (see chapter 7), Massey University (New Zealand) organized a Vice-Chancellor's symposium on the research–teaching Nexus (Suddaby, 2000, 2001). This included:

- External speakers setting out the research evidence and what had been done to develop teaching–research links in three Australian universities (see below and Zubrick, Reid and Rossiter, 2001).

- Workshops run by staff at Massey on the various strategies, course teams and individuals used to link teaching and research.

- Readings on teaching–research relations were distributed in advance of the symposium to all staff who enrolled.

- As Massey has both a main campus and a number of satellite campuses, the main campus event keynotes were videoed and selected workshops presented in roadshows at these other campuses.

Policies and actions were then formulated, supported by the momentum from this event, and such actions are still ongoing. These actions include:

- Publication of key presentations from the symposium and accounts by staff as to how they interlinked teaching and research (Paewai and Suddaby, 2001).

- Twelve policy recommendations to strengthen the nexus were formulated for senior staff to consider. These included:

Establish that research, teaching and the demonstrable ways in which the two interrelate are included in promotions criteria; that new programme proposals contain an environmental impact statement that sets out the way in which the new programme will relate to or affect research; applications for research grants and guidelines for establishing research centres are accompanied by an environmental impact statement that sets out the benefits that the proposed research programme will have for teaching; build our commitment to the interdependence of research and teaching into our planning and reporting framework, including appropriate qualitative and quantitative contextual indicators of our progress.
(Paewai and Suddaby, 2002)

One way to raise awareness and better understand the institutional context is to commission research on aspects of the teaching–research nexus, and then use the research process and results to inform institutional debates and policies. This research can clearly take a variety of forms and be carried out by a range of internal and external staff (and students?). One can consider the nexus as it is perceived by managers and heads of department, as Rowland (1996) did at Sheffield University. One can focus on how different staff in contrasting disciplines perceive the issues (Robertson and Bond, 2001), or of course one can consider the nexus (or lack of) from student views and experiences, as in the studies we have been involved with at Oxford Brookes, and in the case study below from the University of East Anglia. To be effective such research studies need to be rigorously carried out, and clearly benefit from being 'owned' by staff, particularly those whose courses or students are being researched. They must be supported by those centrally responsible for both teaching and research policies. Such combinations are not easy to secure, but this institutional research gives potential insights and legitimacy to subsequent policies and recommendations for practice. Such strategies are also examples of universities showing how they value research by basing their policies on research evidence.

Such research can then lead into and support institutional conferences on teaching–research relations. As an example of this research and linked conference strategy, the University of Wollongong's (Australia) educational development unit initiated a focused research study on practice and perceptions of the nexus in the university. This then provided a platform for a university wide conference that brought national and institutional speakers to raise awareness of the issues in formulating policies to deliver the nexus (http://cedir.uow.edu.au/nexus/).

A RESEARCH PARTNERSHIP AT UEA

The University of East Anglia (UEA) in the UK is a major research university, and its mission statement and Learning and Teaching Strategy emphasizes the value of such research to (undergraduate) students.

A 'short, experimental and relatively small scale study' (Zamorski, 2000: 6), sought to 'investigate the reality of University rhetoric... concerning the relationship of research to teaching' (Zamorski, 2000: 4).

Working with institutional policy makers concerned with the teaching strategy, researchers investigated how staff and students perceived the nexus. The researchers interviewed academic staff. In cooperation with Student Union officers the researchers recruited and trained students to undertake studies of student views, including semi-structured interviews, personal diaries and taking digital photographs of images representing student experience of research.

As with other related studies, a strong theme in the analysis is the complexity of the issues and the danger of focusing on summary highlights. However such summary conclusions include:

- 'Lecturers and students reported many examples and illustrations of what both described as research-led teaching and learning' (Zamorski, 2000: 1).

- 'While students value being close to research, and to the idea of a research university in which they are included, there are many ways in which in practice they feel excluded.... Students have a poor grasp of academic work' (p 1).

- 'Academics reported that the tensions inherent in contemporary academic work could, and sometimes did, fragment and divide what is perceived as a natural and symbiotic relationship between teaching and research. Thus, the benefits of this relationship for students were often diminished' (pp 2–3).

Policies and actions are now being formulated on the basis of this research.

STRATEGY 4: (USE THE BOYER/CARNEGIE ANALYSIS TO) DEVELOP INSTITUTIONAL CONCEPTIONS AND STRATEGIES TO EFFECT TEACHING–RESEARCH LINKS

As institutions differ, they need to develop their own conception and understandings of how they conceive and seek to deliver teaching–research relations. In particular institutional missions and resources will determine the extent to which their focus is on either linking staff discipline based 'discovery research' with student learning, or linking staff scholarly under-standing of their discipline and the scholarship of teaching (that discipline) with student learning.

One of the great strengths of the work by Boyer/Carnegie (see chapter 2) is that they do not offer a procrustean template. Rather they set out a set of intellectual ideas or an academic heuristic and ask others to join with them in challenging, elaborating and developing strategies to deliver them in ways that are appropriate to particular disciplines, departments and institutions (Jenkins, 2000b). In some cases institutions may totally reject these formulations, and certainly the idea of the 'schol-arship of teaching' requires considerable elaboration and may (initially) fit uneasily in the culture of (some) top research universities. Aspects of the Boyer/Carnegie work, in particular the scholarship of service, perhaps reflect US cultural conceptions of university functions. But the strength of the Carnegie heuristic is that all institutions (and national systems) can use it as prompts to develop their own formulation of the connections between the 'scholarship of discovery', the 'scholarship of teaching' and the 'scholarship of integration'. These discussions, and their eventual formulations, enable an institution to develop a shared language to talk about and implement the nexus in ways that suit their institutional culture. There are now many examples of US campuses that have done just that, often supported by national organizations such as the Association for American Higher Education and the Carnegie Foundation (see chapter 7).

However we demonstrate here the value of the Boyer analysis by detailing how it has been applied in the context of three, culturally very different, Australian universities. Institutions worldwide can read this account from their particular national and institutional perspectives.

University of Western Australia, Curtin University of Technology and the University of Ballarat

That the Carnegie work is relevant to other national systems is demonstrated by the research on three Australian institutions (Zubrick, Reid and Rossiter, 2001) http://www.detya.gov.au/highered/eippubs/eip01_2/default.htm. This study demonstrates how three very different institutions have used the Carnegie ideas to develop their own conceptions and strategies to strengthen the teaching–research nexus. The University of Western Australia is a high level research university, or in Australian terms a 'sandstone'; Curtin University of Technology is a more metropolitan applied and professional university, and the University of Ballarat is a small, non-metropolitan institution founded by a merger of formerly separate non-research based institutions. All however see their future as one where teaching–research and scholarship are linked.

The University of Ballarat
The University Council set up a Working Party on 'Developing Scholarship, Research and Student Life'. 'In 1997 the Working Party decided to define and develop its work in terms of Ernest Boyer's four interrelated forms of scholarship... and has sought to define itself as a place where all four scholarships thrive and are valued' (Zubrick, Reid and Rossiter, 2001: 27). More specifically, the policy developments have included:

- Developing academic staff as teacher scholars, 'viewing them as lifelong students of the specialist knowledge of their fields... (and) as life long students of teaching'.

- Involving students in 'field research by students on projects of real significance to the regional community and local enterprises' (p 28).

- Schools and departments have used the Boyer framework to 'incorporate enquiry-based learning, and integrate teaching with research and community service programs in all years of undergraduate study' (p 31).

- Developing strong links with the region, on similar lines to the Carnegie scholarship of service and integration, through the idea of Ballarat as a 'learning city'.

- Development of a Graduate Centre and postgraduate course work based degrees and professional doctorates, partly aimed at regional professionals wanting to study part-time to upgrade their qualifications.

- However, there is a legacy of staff 'whose expectations of academic work are limited to teaching, without necessarily undertaking teaching in scholarly ways' (p 35).

The University of Western Australia
The view of senior staff is that 'wherever possible in a research-intensive university, research should not exist without teaching, and vice versa' (p 38). In 1998, a Teaching–Research Nexus Working Party was set up chaired by a Deputy Vice-Chancellor, with a remit to examine these issues in the light of the Boyer Commission report (University of Stony Brook, 1998) on undergraduate education in research universities, with its call to make research based learning the standard. This working party and related initiatives have:

- Audited the nexus through department submissions on enhancing teaching quality.

- Gathered examples of department and discipline based practice in delivering the link. For example, all fourth year Agriculture students do a major independent research project, in the language of the Boyer Commission, a 'capstone experience'.

- Developed a Teacher Fellowship Scheme for postgraduate students in line with the Boyer Commission's recommendation V111: educate graduate students as apprentice teachers.

- Focused in part on the development of mentoring and support for postgraduate students, in the context of an overall strategy of 25 per cent of students being postgraduates doing research degrees.

- Recognized (as also happened at Ballarat) that many support staff are also involved in scholarship and research, for example, through preparing papers for committees.

- Identified a number of problems in strengthening the nexus at UWA. These included, first, a high number of research only staff; second, the isolation of some research centres from the rest of the department and its curriculum; third:

> in some departments research is highly specialized... approaching the curriculum from an enquiry basis is not an issue. Integrating current research of this type into the undergraduate curriculum is. If strengthening the nexus means helping undergraduate students to appreciate how to ask questions that lead to good answers, it can be done, but not necessarily through illustrations of research in progress.

The fourth problem is balancing the resource demands of postgraduate and undergraduate supervision. Providing (as does the agriculture department) 'undergraduate students with a capstone experience, while maintaining high quality postgraduate student supervision is difficult for some departments. Unless the resources are there, the opportunity to undertake a supervised project would be restricted to the most able or motivated students' (p 440).

Curtin University of Technology
The university was founded in 1987 out of a former College of Advanced Education. Its mission is to be a 'world class university of technology' and it has emphasized the application of research as a source of rooted benefits for the economy, the community and the teaching program. While drawing on the experience of US universities in applying the Boyer model, Curtin's mission has identified teaching and research as being complementary and interlinked, and the linkage is in large measure through scholarship (this echoes Elton's and Barnett's arguments – see chapter 2). The Curtin application of Boyer and its own ideas concerning the nexus has focused in part on:

- Developing teachers' concept of themselves as scholarly resource specialists and professional mentors to students.

- Courses that emphasize students as independent learners.

- Gathering and disseminating examples of enquiry based learning.

- Widening the traditional discovery emphasis to research to a formulation of research that focuses more on impact (on the economy, on teaching...).

- Through an internal research study, recognizing that staff perceive certain barriers to ensuring a positive teaching–research nexus. These included first, 'a limited understanding of the teaching–research nexus among some staff '; second, 'the need for a reward (promotion) system that values a range of scholarly activity'; and third, 'part time and casual staff who have recently acquired doctorates and who may undertake little research or supervision' (p 50) and 'high teaching loads and large classes' (p 54).

- Following this study and in particular the staff views concerning rewards, in 1998 the university started to develop and use portfolios reviewing both teaching and research for promotions, and possibly for appraisal.

- The Research and Development Office is developing a matrix of measures or a common framework to review both teaching and research, so as to 'highlight the nexus between the two areas rather than focusing on the differences' (p 50).

A directive and flexible heuristic

We see this research study of these three institutions as a major tool in helping institutions worldwide in effecting teaching–research connections appropriate to their particular contexts. In particular they show how the Carnegie heuristic is both directive and flexible. It is directive in valuing the diversity of academic roles and seeking their effective integration and it is flexible in enabling different institutions to use and challenge it in ways that empower them and their staff. To anticipate chapter 7, this process is more effective when national funding and review systems enable that diversity.

STRATEGY 5: DEVELOP AND AUDIT TEACHING POLICIES, AND IMPLEMENT STRATEGIES TO STRENGTHEN THE TEACHING–RESEARCH NEXUS

For the nexus to be effective, institutions will perhaps rightfully focus on their teaching strategy, but as we argue in the next section, attention also needs to be directed to their research strategy. In developing an effective teaching strategy to develop the nexus, we suggest that institutions need to decide whether and to what extent the institutional focus is on learning as enquiry, or on linking staff research to student learning, and the degree to which schools and departments have freedoms to develop the nexus in line with their disciplinary cultures.

Two case studies of research based universities in the early stages of developing institutional policies to develop the nexus follow.

University of British Columbia (http://www.vision.ubc.ca/index.html)

UBC (Canada) describes itself as a 'research university'. A recent rethinking of its mission and strategy called 'Trek 2000' set a goal for developing students who graduate with 'strong analytical, problem solving and critical thinking abilities... excellent research-skills'. Trek 2000 set four key strategic goals concerning the undergraduate curriculum to 'Develop learner-centred undergraduate curricula that incorporate research, international, interactive and interdisciplinary components' (University of British Columbia, 2000a: 7). The two that relate to our concerns are specified as follows.

Research based learning
All undergraduate students entering UBC by the year 2003 will, in the course of a four-year degree programme, have a research based learning experience that integrates the many research opportunities at UBC into undergraduate learning. This integration may take many forms, including research seminars, research assistantships, research projects, or research based inquiry and problem solving.

Interactive learning
Students will be exposed to learning that is interactive in process, facilitating two way dialogue and 'hands on' experiences. Personal interactions between student and professor, and between student and student, will be enhanced by new teaching methodologies, research experiences, co-op and work placements and mentoring programs.

The Executive Director in the President's office with a central responsibility for developing these policies, comments: 'These are very general prescriptions, but they are being used by departments and faculties as guidelines in the construction of academic plans, which in turn will have a significant impact on budget allocations and hiring' (Rosengarten, 2000).

The 2000 University Academic Plan (University of British Columbia, 2000b: 21) states that 'every year the budget process approves some academic programs and not others, and approves some hiring plans and not others. From now on the Academic Plan will inform such decisions.... This includes these aims and goals:

- In preparing individual courses or in designing academic programs, we need to ensure that key research skills play an important role in the ways in which we deliver and evaluate (that is, assess – *our edit*) course and program offerings.

- Amongst the various ways we can better integrate research and teaching, the plan encourages a reassessment of our credit and curricular requirements to ensure that undergraduates have opportunities to take research intensive, integrative capstone courses where there is increased credit for their increased effort.

- Students can obtain significant hands on research experience in laboratory, fieldwork and library-based settings and we need to reverse the erosion of this important learning experience.

- We should develop a 'research awareness week' to encourage greater interaction between our undergraduates and the University's top researchers' (pp 8–9).

On the public Web site there are updated reports on the implementation strategies to achieve these goals.

Implementation at Southampton University

To progress its institutional mission, 'a curriculum which communicates the findings of recent research... an ethos of curiosity-driven inquiry', Southampton University's (UK) Learning and Teaching Strategy for the year 2000 includes the following commitments /implementation strategies.

Review of educational practice
'To ask each academic department to develop a written teaching and learning strategy.... The strategy... will include a statement of how research informs its teaching... [and] should address how the department will take forward... teaching within an active research environment' (p 3).

Action plan and department strategies
'To ask each academic department to identify its own action plan.... The development of action plans will be integrated into the framework of quinquennial programme review.... Such a strategy will encompass: the balance in learning strategies between didactic transmission and those which enhance student directed learning' (p 10).

(Department) budgetary groups
'In February each year budgetary groups will be required to submit three year operating plans. Such plans will include progress reports on teaching and research strategies' (p 12).

STRATEGY 6: USE STRATEGIC AND OPERATIONAL PLANNING AND INSTITUTIONAL AUDIT TO STRENGTHEN THE NEXUS

We recall here Gibbs' (2001: 17) analysis of the teaching–research nexus in English HE institutions' learning and teaching strategies, that 'mechanisms through which this nexus might be exploited are not yet articulated.... "Strengthening the nexus" is at present an aspiration rather than a plan.' Thus we recognize that even some of the strategies outlined above, impressive as they are, could result in awareness but limited implementation. At worse, they could be strategies to impress and publicize rather than strategies to deliver. Ways to ensure better implementation include setting specific annual targets for central units, for policies and for their effective implementation at departmental level. (See for example on the public Web site how these are publicly monitored and disseminated at University of British Columbia: http://www.vision.ubc.ca/reports/1999.html.)

One broad strategy to better ensure effective implementation is to use the institutional review and planning process, as follows.

Auditing courses and departments
These should be audited for the various ways and the extent to which they deliver the nexus and for the perceived barriers and effective drivers that departments recommend for institutional planning to strengthen the nexus. Such an audit could be a themed institution wide audit for one year, which provides a basis for planning over a following three-year period.

Building and strengthening the nexus into strategic and operational planning
Many institutions now require schools and departments to detail their strategic plans over a three-year period and annually state their operational plans for that year. As with the University of Southampton case study, developing the teaching–research nexus can be a central requirement for such strategies. Of course, institutions should ensure that such departmental requirements extend to research strategies and not just to the teaching strategy. We shall not shame institutions, but a number of those we have singled out for focusing on their teaching strategy for delivering the nexus have research strategies that completely ignore the nexus.

Providing competitive awards for departments
This should be based on the extent to which departments currently deliver the nexus and have detailed strategies to strengthen it. At the University of Western Australia, departments were encouraged (through significant financial rewards) to develop an electronic portfolio of their teaching strategy that was placed on the university Intranet for other departments to learn from. Most of the portfolios focused on how the department

delivered the nexus. The main prize went to the English department, and as one of the staff commented, preparing the portfolio had 'engaged us as a group of academics collectively and systematically in thinking about our practices... and how teaching and research enabled one another' (Zubrick, Reid and Rossiter, 2001: 124).

UNIVERSITY OF TORONTO: NORTHROP FRYE AWARDS (HTTP://WWW.ALUMNI.UTORONTO.CA/EVENTS/AWARDS/ FRYE.HTM)

Co-sponsored by the University of Toronto Alumni Association and the Provost of the university, the Northrop Frye Awards support university policy to link teaching and research. Annually, one individual faculty member and one department or division are recognized (including financially) with the award for demonstrating exemplary and innovative ways of linking teaching and research.

For example the department award for 1999 went to the departments of Botany and Zoology for their jointly taught first year biology course, to over 15,000 students over the past 10 years. The university Web site states that 'It has served as a model for biology courses at other universities. Some of U of T's top researchers teach the course, lecturing within their areas of expertise and presenting undergraduate students with the very latest in biological research. *In labs, students are encouraged to observe, ask questions and design experiments to test hypotheses; in other words, they are taught to think like researchers'* (our emphasis).

STRATEGY 7: DEVELOP CURRICULUM REQUIREMENTS

While respecting disciplinary and course team autonomy and creativity, institutions can further the teaching–research nexus by requiring, or simply encouraging, certain structures that ensure students experience a research and enquiry based curriculum. These might include the following.

First year requirements
Certain North American universities have guaranteed the provision of, or encouraged all first year students to take, at least one course in a small class enquiry format with assessment that develops high level learning (Barff, 1995). At Northwestern University (Illinois, USA) all freshers in arts and sciences are required to take two seminars, which are discussion oriented courses limited to 15 students introducing them to the intellectual life of the university and helping to develop the skills of good scholarship. Seminars are offered by every department and by several interdisciplinary programs,

and departments with heavy enrolments may be given special funds to enable them to offer such fresher seminars. See http://www.cas.north-western.edu/ug/fsemw2000.html.

The University of Southern Carolina (http://www.sc.edu/fye/) focuses on supporting policies that support 'students in transition' (National Resource Centre for the First Year Experience and Students in Transition). Many US institutions have developed such special programme and curriculum requirements that focus on the first year experience of developing enquiry learning. Such programmes illustrate the Boyer Commission's (University of Stony Brook, 1998) call to ensure 'the first year of a university experience... [provides] a firm grounding in inquiry-based learning' (see chapters 2 and 4).

Undergraduate and postgraduate programme requirements
While in many institutions course requirements are decided at department level, in others broad requirements are specified at institutional level, particularly in those where modular or credit structures shape or even determine parameters for local implementation. In such institutions, central programme requirements can support the nexus, but hopefully in ways that give due freedom for course team creativity, and respect disciplinary differences in delivering the nexus. In 2001, Oxford Brookes University initiated a major restructuring of its institution-wide Undergraduate Modular Programme, in particular changing from its previous three-term structure to a two-semester system. The institution saw in such a fundamental course restructuring an opportunity to require all course teams to develop broad key requirements over interdisciplinary, reflective 'capstone' requirements, and in particular to require all course teams to 'demonstrate how the linkages between research and learning are realized, in particular in the four module credits that comprise the module credits that comprise the compulsory honours element of the course, but also more generally' (Perkins, 2002: 2).The McMaster case study below is that of an institutional change process that started from problem based professional programmes, was then taken across the institution with first year inquiry based courses and then up into advanced courses.

**Inquiry courses at McMaster University
(http://www.mcmaster.ca/learning/resources/inquiry.htm)**

McMaster University (Ontario, Canada) has an international reputation for innovative courses in engineering and medicine that are problem based. Recently the university developed a curricular (and faculty development) change strategy called the 'McMaster Inquiry Project' to develop enquiry-based courses across the university. The project Web site states:

a central goal will be to inculcate the concept of 'student as active learner' throughout the entire undergraduate experience. Our undergraduates should not learn primarily as passive recipients of information, but as active participants in their education in order to better develop critical thinking and communication skills....

The skills that are most widely sought in university graduates – the capacities to research and analyze complex problems and to communicate easily and effectively about them – are fundamental to all disciplines. The trend to emphasize the development of analysis and inquiry skills began in professional schools and is now spreading to other disciplines. At McMaster, we have defined these skills to include:

- the ability to ask good questions;
- the ability to determine what needs to be learned in order to answer those questions;
- the ability to identify appropriate resources for learning;
- the ability to use resources effectively and to report on what was learned;
- the ability to self evaluate.

Implementation includes:

- Providing an opportunity for all McMaster undergraduates to take an Inquiry Seminar in their first year of university.
- Ensur[ing]... students have the opportunity to take at least one inquiry-based course in each subsequent year of their university education.
- Ensur[ing] that all senior-year undergraduates registered in honours programs have the opportunity to participate in a research program individually supervised by a McMaster professor.

Implementation is supported by selected staff from across the university working in project teams to develop their skills in teaching this way and such pedagogy is now central to a course aimed at newly appointed faculty.

Graduate profile and graduation requirements
One of the suggestions of a group of UK academics seeking to develop teaching–research links was that institutions, and 'policy and funding drivers... need to foster culture change through the introduction of a

graduate standard which includes a requirement for research skills awareness' (Southampton Institute, 2000: 14). This is now supported by UK national quality assurance requirements (see Chapter 7).

Thesis, dissertation and synoptic requirements

As we argued in chapter 4, curricula that include dissertations or synoptic units as a central feature of the undergraduate experience are key strategies for course teams that seek to link teaching and research. Institutions can ensure that this happens through requirements such as the following. 'To obtain an honours degree, a student must gain at least two module credits from project, dissertation or synoptic modules' (Oxford Brookes Undergraduate Modular Course Regulations). These requirements, which generally focus on students doing some independent enquiry, are common for honours classification in the UK and elsewhere, reminding us that there is much already in place in national systems and in individual institutions that fosters teaching–research connections.

Similarly in the United States there has been increased interest and development of institutional requirements for capstone or synoptic style courses, which focus on integrating student knowledge of (research and scholarship) of their discipline developed through their degree. Indeed the University of Southern Carolina, the national centre focusing on the first year experience (see earlier) has now developed a related focus on linking institutions that have introduced or are considering introducing such '401 Courses' (http://www.sc.edu/fye/401/university401.htm).

STRATEGY 8: REVIEW THE TIMETABLE

One key lever to moving an institution to link teaching and research is to radically revise the timetable, and in effect the curriculum, to create periods of concentrated study on a central topic. Staff know the most effective way to get research done is to have concentrated time on a topic, be that sabbaticals, terms with limited or no formal teaching, or the summer vacation. So ensuring that students have time to focus on the complexities of an issue may be (in part) effected through radically changing the college timetable. Most institutions operate what Hewton (1977: 79) called the 'dispersed' timetable, where 'activities (lectures, seminars, laboratories and so on) are represented by fairly short periods of time scattered over a weekly timetable. For most students the week, and probably the day, consists of a varied and unrelated set of events.' The one hour block (leavened by longer laboratory sessions) and the pattern of students studying three or four, at best partly related, courses or modules is well established. There are evident reasons for this structure: for example, ensuring choice, curricular variety and so on, but it needs to be reviewed as an institution seeks to strengthen the teaching–research nexus. Certainly those of us who teach field based disciplines from architecture to zoology know they enable an intense intellectual experience, and often involve students doing research based projects over a number of days. Is this concentrated pattern of learning one that all disciplines could use to strengthen teaching–research connections? At Oxford Brookes the institution moved from the dominant one hour block to a dominant four hour timetable for a variety of reasons, including that of enabling part-time students to attend. But anecdotal evidence suggests that one key result was a shift from lecture based teaching to much more active methods.

There are now a range of examples of institutions, departments and course teams radically revising the timetable to enable more inquiry based learning. Perhaps the classic example is that of physics at MIT (see case study below), partly because it was the subject of a major research study. Other examples include:

- The School of Computer Studies and Mathematics at the University of Sunderland, interspersed the normal fragmented timetable with workshop courses. These courses lasted from two to five days, and in these workshops student groups focused on a single exercise (Thompson, 1988).

- Beloit College (Wisconsin, USA), and other biology departments in US liberal arts and science colleges developing research or inquiry based curricula, are 'moving from four (separate) lecture hours and a lab block (generally over five days) to meeting in the lab for three two hour blocks. Both the quantity and quality of learning are intensified' (Jungck, 1997: 36).

- Colorado and Cornell Colleges have switched to a '4–1–4 or 4–4 (hour) approach to create a time where students can focus on just one subject, allowing greater opportunity for long-term fieldwork and intensive lab projects' (Jungck, 1997: 36).

PHYSICS THROUGH CONCENTRATED STUDY AT MIT

In 1968, an experimental physics course was taught at Massachusetts Institute of Technology (MIT) that involved some 20 students working with one instructor over five to six weeks. For these students it replaced the normal course timetable of two lectures and one seminar. It, and related curricula experiments, was evaluated by Malcolm Parlett, an educational researcher and evaluator (Parlett and King, 1971). Aspects relevant to this book include:

- MIT institutional policy enabled this experiment by the institutional Educational Committee being empowered to 'approve limited educational experiments... [that] depart from faculty regulations and MIT administrative procedures' (p 2).

- The course was not the usual course taught intensively. Rather the instructor saw the change of timetable as enabling a total rethink of the curriculum, which centred on students working individually and collectively on laboratory projects in a way that strongly parallels the contemporary Roskilde curriculum (see earlier description).

- Students felt that 'overall they had learned far more physics than in previous courses they had taken; and that their knowledge was richer, more diverse, more interesting, more interconnected and unified. The instructor found this method of instruction *more rewarding, and a more efficient and natural way of communicating his knowledge of physics'* (pp 23, 28) (emphasis added).

- In comments that relate strongly to the discussion of student motivation in chapter 3, 'many of the students suggested that the question "How hard did you work?" was inapplicable. Since they enjoyed the studying and activities so much, they did not see it as hard, and in a number of instances not as work' (p 14).

STRATEGY 9: DEVELOP SPECIAL PROGRAMMES

Students differ in abilities and motivations about research. While our perspective is to widen and deepen the numbers of students gaining from a research based education, is it sensible to recognize that research based education is most appropriate only for selected students? Clearly there are political, ethical, cultural and financial issues that need be considered in coming to such a conclusion.

Nationally (see chapter 7) there are differences between elitist systems such as the UK's which presume that all students entering higher education should experience research, and more mass systems such as the USA's that see such research based education as being only appropriate at graduate level or to selected undergraduate students. Such is the perspective of the various honours programmes emphasizing research based enquiry that are a (an increasing?) feature of major US research universities: partly in response to the Boyer/Carnegie critique of research universities. Effectively these programmes seek to present the small class and residential components of small rich liberal arts colleges like Hampshire College, but in the context of a major research university, and where working with research based staff is central to the undergraduate experience. The case study of Rutgers below is one of a number of such programmes. Viewing the Web sites of such programmes revealed these general features:

- High academic entry requirements and requirements to maintain a high grade average. 'You have to maintain a 3.5 GPA [grade point average] to stay in the college' (honors programme, University of Arizona).

- Small class sizes. 'Average class size is 18 students' (honors programme, University of Arizona).

- Specialist residential units. 'A superb residential living and learning community composed of talented and highly motivated students' (honors programme, Colorado State University).

- Research opportunities. 'Increased faculty to student interaction through research opportunities, independent honors course in the department major, and the honors thesis or project' (honors programme, Colorado State University). 'Research grants totalling US $40,000 available to undergraduates each year' (honors programme, University of Arizona).

- Graduate and professional school entry. 'Close interaction with a faculty member and a finished piece of serious research are among the most powerful credentials to graduate or professional school' (University of Georgia).

For those of us in the UK, New Zealand and elsewhere where there is a strong view that a research or dissertation experience is central to an undergraduate degree, such programmes may be seen as favouring the few and neglecting the many. Perhaps, though, such programmes are a more realistic recognition of what is possible, given current funding for HE and the more diverse student abilities and orientation or motivation towards research. Perhaps while requiring research based experiences for all, preference does need to be given to those students with strong research interests and aptitudes. We do consider that non-US institutions may want to consider how aspects of these programmes could be adapted to their institutional and cultural context.

Programmes like the one at Rutgers reinforce the central theme of this chapter: that if institutions want to ensure that either selected or all students benefit from research, then institutional planning on a range of issues is required.

Rutgers University: an institutional focus on undergraduate research (http://www.rutgers.edu/urru)

Rutgers (New Jersey, USA) is a Research 1 university, that is, it is a research focused university. To define and deliver the special characteristics, and the added value students should get from studying at such an institution, Rutgers initiated the following measures (Forman, 2000).

An undergraduate research roundtable: a series of meetings across the campus at which faculty were asked to 'consider the goals of an undergraduate research university experience' and to 'advise the administration on the type of development that was needed in this area'.

A general curriculum review of the whole undergraduate programme emerged from the roundtable and led to:

- A set of learning goals for undergraduate programmes, some of which did focus on the research process, for example, 'understanding scientific modes on inquiry'. Programmes and faculties then developed these more specifically into courses and requirements.

- A small grants programme which supported faculty-initiated curriculum development projects with a (partial) focus on developing students' research skills and research methodology.

- An undergraduate research university experience brochure was sent to all students at the beginning of their second year, to orientate them in what it means to be a student at a research university, and to outline the benefits to them of getting involved in research based programmes.

- An undergraduate research Web site which provides lists of research based opportunities that students can search by campus or town, by discipline, and type of research activity. The site also gives details on entry requirements and so on.

- The Rutgers University Undergraduate Research Fellows Program (1997) competitive faculty initiated bids. Funds have all to be used to support student involvement in faculty organized research projects: money can be used to send students to national meetings to present results and so on. The criteria for awards are: 'first, depth of student involvement in project, second, the value of the educational experience for the student, third, the extent of faculty supervision, and fourth, the nature of anticipated student products arising from the project'. Students get the title of 'Undergraduate Research Fellow'. The programme is supported by a range of corporate sponsors.

- Rutgers undergraduate research weeks (initiated 1998) are a series of events celebrating and publicizing what undergraduates have achieved in their research.

- *The Rutgers Scholar* (initiated 1999) is an electronic journal publicizing collaborative (students with staff) research at Rutgers.

While most of this involves faculty working with upper level students on individual or small group projects, these initiatives also led to, and supported, projects that sought to embed research based approaches in introductory courses. Two current (2000) initiatives are:

- Addressing undergraduate research in introductory courses for non-majors, by introducing a research element to (large) introductory courses.

- Undergraduate research preparation workshops for first and second year students are workshop based courses that develop students' understanding of research, and in effect prepare them to apply for the Undergraduate Research Fellows Program. (This project is supported by the National Science Foundation: for NSF details see chapter 7.)

If institutional teaching and research strategies are to be interlinked then this requires action from both sides: that is, through both the teaching and research strategies. Perhaps it requires (more fundamentally) strategies and planning processes that do not see teaching and research as 'binary' categories.

STRATEGY 10: DEVELOPING RESEARCH TO SUPPORT THE NEXUS

The three-part, interrelated family of academic plans comprising the research plan, the teaching and learning plan and the community outreach plan form a dynamic sequence of interlocking plans at university, school centre and office level.... The promotion of research is the basis of the educational mission at Macquarie which highlights scholarly teaching at the cutting edge of knowledge. (Macquarie University, 2000: 1–5)

Statements such as this from Macquarie University (Australia) are significant in giving a strategic direction to better ensuring that there are effective linkages in intent, policy, structure and practice between teaching and research. But such statements and strategic directions clearly need to be developed through operational plans, academic structures and so on.

We fear that those institutions in the UK which have recently claimed to link teaching and research will as yet have little or no measures to ensure such effective integration in their teaching, or certainly in their research strategies. Gibbs' (2001) analysis of 133 English teaching and learning strategies demonstrated that only 2 per cent of them made explicit links with their research strategies, and we suspect that was mainly in terms of pedagogic research and not in terms of the discipline based research discussed here. To anticipate the next chapter, that may in part be a product of the external funding for research.

Yet the research by Colbeck on two contrasting institutions clearly demonstrated the critical role of institutional (and departmental) research policies and cultures as to what 'counts' as research, as profoundly affecting whether staff can integrate teaching and research. (See chapter 2.) She concluded that:

> University policies for evaluating faculty research provided 'Cosmopolitan State' (the lower ranked 'Comprehensive' university) with more opportunities than their 'Vantage University' colleagues (a Carnegie Research 1 university) to integrate classroom orientated teaching with research. The 'Cosmopolitan State Faculty Handbook' (which defined research activities for funding and for promotion) began with articles or creative work published in refereed journals but also included textbooks, newspaper articles, and creative work published in popular media.
>
> In effect, Vantage research evaluation policies limited research to the scholarship of inquiry (Boyer, 1990), whereas Cosmopolitan State policies embraced scholarships of inquiry, integration, application and teaching. *The broader the university definition of what counts for research, the more faculty are able to integrate research and classroom-oriented teaching.*
> (Colbeck, 1998: 660–61, emphasis in original)

It would be interesting to replicate Gibbs' analysis of institutional teaching strategies for university research strategies, and of course in any national system, not just the UK. To what extent do these research strategies demonstrate that a (central) aim of research is to support the nexus, and most of all, to what extent do they reveal clear operational plans and targets to promote effectively teaching–research links at institutional, department and course team levels? We know of few institutional research policies that are explicitly aimed at the level of operating strategies to secure such teaching–research synergies. We hope that we are wrong, and that others will write about how that is achieved or attempted at their institution. Here are two case studies of institutional research policies, from very different institutional (and national) contexts that seek to promote the nexus.

PEDAGOGIC IMPACT STATEMENTS AT EARLHAM COLLEGE

Earlham College, Indiana, USA (a private Quaker based liberal arts college) initiated a requirement that internal requests for research support include a pedagogic impact statement: 'a description of the impact that the research is likely to have on teaching…. [One of the Deans who developed this system argued] let's talk about teaching and research at a point when something actually can be done to insure that they complement and reinforce each other' (Bakker, 1995: B3).

PERFORMANCE INDICATORS AT AUCKLAND

As part of the institutional preparation for the audit of its teaching-research nexus, the University of Auckland developed over 50 performance indicators for departments and the institution at large to discuss and assess how it was progressing the link. These were then published in the *Academic Audit Portfolio* (University of Auckland, 2000), for the national audit of teaching–research links (see chapters 2 and 7, and note that John Hattie, whose research has significantly shaped this publication and our collective understanding of teaching–research relations, was part of the group developing these indicators). Performance indicators for research policy (p 59) included these measures:

- Research and its link with teaching, should be in the context of a public research management policy and associated plan.

- Formal contractual responsibility to engage in teaching and research.

- Provision for staff to change their teaching–research proportions from time to time by agreement, moving between 20 per cent teaching and 80 per cent research, and 80 per cent teaching and 20 per cent research.

- The degree to which research grants are sought with reference to teaching.

- Evidence of research carried out into teaching methods and learning strategies in various disciplines by staff in those disciplines.

- The degree to which there is joint teaching and research use of equipment, other researchers or research activities.

- The degree to which research proposals required to indicate any expected positive (or negative) effects on teaching.

- Ensure that best researchers teach across all year levels.

- Evidence of the research culture on teaching and learning.

- How does the institution ensure that the teaching and learning are different from what would occur if there were no research and how is this difference measured?

The public report of the ensuing audit by the national Academic Audit Unit (2000: 14) commented on these indicators: 'The AAU recognises the inherent difficulties in measuring the teaching–research nexus. Many staff expressed the view that the Kips (key performance indicators) being developed to assess the teaching–research link seem appropriate, a view shared by the panel.'

Other strategies we think could be considered by institutional research strategies include:

- Explicitly requiring departments to state how their research strategy supports or interlinks with their teaching strategy and their operational plans to strengthen the nexus, but giving departments considerable freedom to devise strategies they consider appropriate.

- Explicitly targeting proportions of research income to support specific courses (and the staff teaching them), particularly those at postgraduate level.

- Requiring all departments to allocate a percentage of research funds, staff research time, sabbaticals and so on, to support the production of student textbooks and learning software.

- Allocating a percentage of research and teaching funds to support all full time (and part-time?) staff as scholars in their discipline and in the teaching of their discipline, and perhaps ensuring that all have periodic involvement in 'discovery' research projects. This focus is particularly important in those institutions outside the research elite, for here only a limited percentage of staff will be 'research active' in discovery research.

- Periodically reviewing research facilities and equipment in terms of how students could appropriately benefit from such institutional resources, while of course recognizing that their central function is to support high-level staff research.

- Allocating a certain proportion of research funding to support student research initiatives, be they research projects, attendance at conferences, or student journals as detailed in the case study in the box.

STUDENT RESEARCH JOURNALS

A number of US institutions and consortia of institutions have journals, often Web based, where selected (undergraduate and/or postgraduate) students present their research. (One recent Web search found some 100 such journals in the United States, though many of them seemed effectively to be 'out of print' (Poinsot, 2001).) They are particularly prominent in research based universities and geared to the sciences.

Examples of such journals that are current as of December 2001 included:

- *Journal of Young Investigators* (consortium of several universities) http://jyi.org

- *Journal of Undergraduate Study and Independent Research* (JUSIR) http://www.jusir.org

- *Caltech Undergraduate Research Journal*, http://curj.caltech.edu

- *Yale: YSEA Undergraduate Journal*, http://www.yale.edu/ysea/journal.html.

The *Journal of Young Investigators* (a peer reviewed undergraduate science journal) is particularly innovative in not only publishing student research papers but also involving students in the refereeing and editing processes. A recent development is the appointment to the journal of staff scientists who, working with volunteer mentors from the national and institutional science community, support students in writing for external publication. It sees its particular goal as being to 'introduce students to the exercise of communicating their research, reviewing and being reviewed by peers, and other aspects of publishing and disseminating information. This journal is in large measure based at a consortia of institutions including Duke, Swathmore and Georgetown, but is also supported by national organizations including the National Science Foundation, Glaxo Wellcome Inc and *Science Magazine*.

This model could be, and has been, adapted outside the US system. Indeed in 2001, a student journal called *Biologos* directed at the biological sciences was initiated at the University of Rennes in France (http://biologos.univ-rennes1.fr/) and another *Origin: A journal of undergraduate research in the biological sciences* (http://www.chester.ac.uk/origin/), supported by the Biosciences Subject Centre, Chester College (UK). Institutions such as (in the UK) the Royal Literary Fund (http://www.learndev.qmw.ac.uk/elss/rlfinfo.htm), which helps writers financially by having them (on a part-time basis) support student writing. This might be directed to encouraging student writing on their research where this is clearly linked to institutional research policies.

STRATEGY 11: ENSURE LINKS BETWEEN RESEARCH CENTRES AND STAFF SCHOLARSHIP WITH THE CURRICULUM AND STUDENT LEARNING

In many universities research is in part concentrated in research centres. There are evident arguments for this in terms of the organization of research: developing a critical mass of researchers and so on. In terms of institutions that wish to develop an effective teaching–research nexus, the evident danger is that such research centres may have little or no beneficial impact on teaching. Rather they may have the unintended consequence of driving apart teaching and research. While it is recognized that many institutions will want to concentrate and develop research through such centres, ways to ensure they can also support the teaching–research nexus include:

- Build the nexus into the requirements for establishing (research) centres. For example at the University of Western Australia, the nexus is one of the four expected features of centres. The university guidelines state: 'A centre should enhance the teaching–research nexus in clearly identifiable ways through its activities or through the activities of individual members. In particular, research staff in centres should be encouraged to contribute to teaching and/or supervision of students enrolled in cognate departments' (University of Western Australia, 2001: 2).

- Make one of their functions the teaching of selected postgraduate courses, perhaps particularly those interdisciplinary courses that cut across department boundaries.

- Provide opportunities for mainstream teaching staff to have periodic research roles or sabbaticals in the centre.

- Ensure that selected centre staff play roles as consultants to course teams and have limited teaching roles in academic departments.

- 'Establishing formal organizational connections... that allow opportunities for senior undergraduates and honours students to have "affiliations" during their studies. This would assist able undergraduate students to experience intensive research in operation as well as provide an important student and teaching link for staff who may hold research-only appointments' (Zubrick, Reid and Rossiter, 2001: 81).

**STRATEGY 12: ENSURE THE NEXUS IS CENTRAL TO POLICIES
ON INDUCTING AND DEVELOPING NEW STAFF AND TO
STRATEGIES TO SUPPORT THE PROFESSIONAL
DEVELOPMENT OF ESTABLISHED STAFF**

Institutions can shape effective teaching–research connections through
how they induct new staff, for it is at these initial stages that such training is
often compulsory. There are also opportunities in courses and developments for established staff. More specifically:

- Graduate research and teaching assistant programmes can include activities and requirements which get these novitiate staff to explore ways to
  help students learn from their current specialized (doctoral) research.
  For example, at Stanford University (http://sll.stanford.edu/projects/
  i-rite/) the programme CREATE works with doctoral students on writing
  and communicating their research to non-specialists, including starting
  students in their disciplines (Marincovitch and Reis, 2000). It is
  important to note that certainly in the United States, there is a growing
  concern that many doctoral programmes exclusively educate students
  for specialist discovery research. These staff then move to other institutions with more diverse missions and into roles with a strong teaching
  emphasis. Therefore institutions may want to re-examine their doctoral
  programmes to ensure they support postgraduate students to seek more
  integrated training and careers, and thereby aid their future employability and support the nexus in institutions and at a national level.

- Accredited courses on teaching for new and mid-career academics can
  include activities, including issues of curriculum design, about how such
  staff can ensure students benefit from staff research. Recently the
  Institute for Learning and Teaching (ILT) accredited course at Brookes
  has been changed to include a workshop on fostering
  teaching–research links. The anecdotal evidence is that for many course
  participants this was intellectually exciting and one that helped them
  explore ways of integrating their roles. (Yet perhaps for some it seemed
  irrelevant or premature.) Similarly at the University of Waikato, New
  Zealand, the University Certificate in Tertiary Teaching now has an
  early module on 'The Scholarship of Tertiary Teaching' which helps
  staff to see links between their teaching and research (Haigh, 2000),
  and recently a similar module has been introduced into the Massey
  course (Suddaby and St George, 2002). At the University of Strathclyde
  (UK), as part of an accredited course on teaching and learning in
  higher education, there are modules on academic writing. These ask
  faculty to consider how writing can support student learning and how

staff can develop themselves as academic writers in their discipline. Murray (2001: 41), who teaches these modules, concludes that 'a formal course on academic writing is one way of developing teaching and scholarship in an integrated fashion... [for as a result] a dialectic can be established between teaching and research roles and between students' and teachers' writing.'

- However, we note that Kreber and Cranton (2000: 224) take a slightly different position. They do argue that faculty development units must shift from a focus on teaching skills programmes to a more scholarly and teaching–research integrated approach. However they argue that 'a more meaningful approach might be to allow more inexperienced faculty to specialise in one area, teaching or research, in the early years, and to foster integration of professorial responsibilities to once they have had the opportunity to develop expertise.'

- For such staff started in their career, integration in terms of staff development can be fostered by institutional appraisal systems, by encouragement, by the requirements on course teams and departmental research strategies and so on that we have detailed above, and perhaps most of all through the institutional faculty award system.

STRATEGY 13: ENSURE TEACHING–RESEARCH LINKS ARE CENTRAL TO POLICIES ON PROMOTION AND REWARD

There is now strong research evidence both on the importance of promotion, tenure and staff reward policies in influencing institutional cultures and practices towards teaching quality (Wright and O'Neill, 1995), and how most institutional policies are seen as promoting research and neglecting teaching (for example, Ramsden *et al*, 1998). While it is recognized that staff motivations are varied (see chapter 3), if institutions really want to link teaching and research then this clearly needs to be supported by the way that promotions policies are framed and implemented. As Hattie and Marsh (1996: 533) state in their review of the research evidence, 'The aim is to provide *rewards* not only for better teaching or for better research but *for demonstrations of the integration between teaching and research*' (emphasis added).

Clearly if that perspective is accepted then institutions need to review and revise their current promotion and appraisal policies for all levels of academic staff. The case study of Auckland indicates one institution's early thoughts on performance indicators for institutional monitoring. Some institutions may want to support staff with specialized roles, but ensure that the linkage is one aspect built into promotion for research or teaching focused staff. This will vary by institutional mission, and to return to the research evidence in chapter 2, whether the institution is promoting integration at the level of the individual member of staff, or at the level of the course team and so on.

PERFORMANCE INDICATORS FOR PROMOTIONS AT AUCKLAND

- Is an explicit teaching–research link included in the criteria for both teaching and research, both at appointment and promotion?

- How do promotion committees reward the links (not merely rewarding good teaching or good research)?

- Reduction in the insecurity of untenured staff to succeed by primarily engaging in research (University of Auckland, 2000: 59).

STRATEGY 14: ENSURE EFFECTIVE SYNERGIES BETWEEN UNITS, COMMITTEES AND STRUCTURES FOR TEACHING AND RESEARCH

Most institutions now have a unit that works with staff to improve their teaching through courses, conferences and so on. Most have similar units and officers to promote research (and probably consultancy). In institutions there are committees concerned with teaching and committees concerned with research. However on most campuses these are physically and organizationally separate, perhaps with good reason.

If an institution really intends to link teaching and research then it should consider how such units and committees are conceived and organized. Could more effective synergies be developed through reshaping, merging or co-locating functions of such units, or through periodic consultations and projects to ensure such synergies?

Therefore Southampton Institute (UK) had a special meeting of the teaching and research committees to progress institutional and department strategies to exploit the potential linkages between the responsibilities of these two committees. The Institute is surely to be commended for such a meeting, but perhaps the central question we all have to ask is, why is this so unusual that it needs bringing to our attention?

'JOINED-UP THINKING' AND STRATEGY AT SOUTHAMPTON INSTITUTE

Southampton Institute (UK) had a special meeting (in April 2000) of its two committees with separate responsibilities for institutional policies: for teaching the Academic Development Committee, and for research the Research and Scholarship Committee (Latham, 2001). Significantly, this was a recent change in name to add the word 'scholarship' to the previous Research Committee. This meeting:

- Built on and progressed work the institution had been doing in developing 'horizontal strategies', to effectively link the strategies being developed in the faculties.

- Two horizontal strategies were first, on research and scholarship, and second, on learning, teaching and curriculum development.

- The special meeting had the explicit aim of exploring the potential links between the two strategies, with the aim of producing practical outcomes to realize these linkages.

- Some of those attending were known to each other at most by name. Seeing their roles concerning teaching or research revealed they did not really know each other, and that is something we can all recognise!

- The first part of the meeting consisted of presentations on the two strategies.

- The second part was led by an outside facilitator (Graham Gibbs) who presented a range of issues for discussion: this soon turned into an open lively discussion on differing views on teaching–research relations.

- The earlier aim of the meeting to produce 'practical outcomes' was soon seen as premature. Open discussion was what was needed at this stage.

- After the meeting, a working party with members from both committees produced a draft bridging paper between the two strategies.

- Draft objectives to implement such a bridging strategy include: 'To raise the level of debate on the evidence of the benefits to student learning of explicit links with staff scholarship and research; To offer a greater level of support to staff in increasing their engagement in scholarship and research as a means to benefit student learning; To encourage innovative approaches to course design and to working with undergraduate students in order to create circumstances in which the benefits of staff research and scholarship are shared effectively' (Southampton Institute, 2000: 3).

- These outline strategies are now being further considered, in particular through a review of the Institute's research strategy (Latham, 2001).

Neil Haigh, an educational developer at the University of Waikato, (New Zealand) recounts how as a result of being a member of a working party on teaching–research relations in his university, and reading Boyer and others, his:

> Staff development agenda... has become more holistic... because of my greater appreciation of the interrelationships that potentially exist between the various activities that constitute the core of academic work.... This means, for example, that I consider teaching development should not be addressed in isolation from other aspects of academic development.
> (Haigh, 2000)

The working party on teaching–research relations at Waikato included staff from various roles and committees across the university. One of the outcomes was the *Strategic Plan for Research and Postgraduate Studies* (University of Waikato, 1999). For a research strategy this is notable for its explicit discussion of teaching–research relations, and how schools might foster such linkages.

STRATEGY 15: LINK WITH RELATED UNIVERSITY STRATEGIES

For all institutions, linking teaching and research will be but one of a range of strategies, even for those institutions where it is right at the core of the institutional mission. Institutional policy makers need to ensure, or at least consider how to ensure, synergy between strategies for linking teaching and research with other related strategies.

Penn State University, the University of Michigan and the University of Wisconsin, Madison (USA) have all developed strong programmes similar to that at Rutgers detailed earlier, but these are all explicitly designed in part to meet the institutional priorities of meeting the needs of under-represented groups and widening cultural and ethnic access (Elowson and Gregerman, 2001). The case study from Warwick illustrates this general strategy of linking diverse and potentially unrelated strategies. We do recognize that in this book we have not focused on the critical role of the university library and its policies in supporting the nexus. For the start of a such a policy, see the Toronto Library Web site (http://www.library.utoronto.ca/news/undergrad_services/report/chap_2. htm) which reports on how the library is taking forward in its support for undergraduate students, the institutional vision and commitment to 'a research university in which teaching and research are intimately linked, in which communities of scholars participate in international networks at the frontiers of their areas of study'. Hopefully even this brief mention of the critical role of libraries points to the diverse agents and policies that need to be linked through institutional policies and structures to support the nexus.

LINKING TEACHING, RESEARCH AND C&IT STRATEGIES AT THE UNIVERSITY OF WARWICK

The University of Warwick (UK) describes itself as a 'research-focused university'. A current project to embed C&IT in teaching seeks to ensure this initiative supports teaching-research linkages (Roach, Blackmore and Dempster, 2001). It does this through:

● *Title.* The project is called TELRI (Technology Enhanced Learning in Research-Led Institutions). http://www.warwick.ac.uk/telri/. (It is a nationally supported project through the Teaching and Learning Technology Programme.)

● *Linked institutions.* The partner institutions are those that staff will see as being like themselves, committed to high-level research: Birmingham, Durham, Oxford and Southampton.

● *Pedagogic model.* The project team has developed a pedagogic model (focusing around issues of curriculum design and assessment) that promotes inquiry based learning.

● *Relevant software.* The software that is being used in the project is seen as being supportive of inquiry based teaching.

STRATEGY 16: PARTICIPATE IN NATIONAL PROGRAMMES

The Warwick case study is also an example of how an institution can use national programmes, particularly those that provide resources, to affect institutional policies to link teaching and research. For though university funds and resources go into that programme at Warwick, the national funding gives key resources to bring about institutional change. The Rutgers set of linked strategies, set out earlier, also has a fund to which staff can bid to support any bids to national programmes such as the National Science Foundation. The wider issue of how national policies (and programmes) can support the nexus is developed in chapter 7.

STRATEGY 17: SUPPORT IMPLEMENTATION AT SCHOOL AND DEPARTMENT LEVEL

In the introduction to this chapter we referred to Burton Clark's view (Clark, 1993a) that the role of the institution in shaping teaching–research relations is formative (that is, setting a general context), with key enactment being at the department level. We hope we have demonstrated in this chapter the critical role of, and the wide range of, possible institutional policy levers.

Most of these do need enacting at departmental level and adapting to departmental and disciplinary cultures. Institutions can support that process through a range of measures including:

- events where departments share good practice and discuss how they are dealing with problems in implementation;

- ensuring (as do the University of Southampton and University of British Columbia institutional strategies referred to above) that departments are required through strategy documents, and in particular budget allocations, to implement the overall strategy through the processes of internal quality assurance;

- recognizing, and celebrating, that departments (and course teams) will implement this in very different ways in accordance with local conditions including disciplinary cultures.

We now turn to that critical level of the academic department, and how it can support the nexus.

6

Organizing the department to link teaching and research

We found little evidence to suggest that synergies between teaching and research were managed or promoted at departmental or institutional level.... There were some attempts to manage teaching and research workloads in departments, partly to allow more time for research. Some strategies may be having the unintended consequence of driving research and teaching apart for some staff.
(JM Consulting, 2000: 36)

Research, teaching and study can exist in not so splendid isolation, with full time research staff in one corner, some teaching staff off in one corner and only slightly guided, if at all, by the results of recent research, and students studying in another corner, with codified text in hand but out of the sight of research activities and peering at distant teachers as if through the wrong end of a telescope.
(Clark, 1993b: 301)

INTRODUCTION

In his book on academic leadership, Paul Ramsden (1998: X11) emphasizes the key role of the academic department and leadership at that level. He states: 'Simply put, research activity and productivity, and the quality of teaching and learning, are influenced for better or worse by the way a department is managed or led.'

Perhaps, most fundamentally, the department is often where teaching and research resources, including staff time and roles are most directly organized. In addition, if we see the research on teaching and research relations as showing the importance of the discipline in shaping that relationship (see chapter 2), then the department is a critical unit of analysis, for this is generally the level at which disciplinary communities within institutions are organized. There is also research evidence that departments play a critical role in shaping teaching and research cultures in staff (Austin, 1996; Volkwein and Carbone, 1994). It is for these reasons that Clark (1993a) sees the department as where teaching–research relations are enacted. This chapter considers particular strategies that departments and their policy makers can use to enact a positive teaching–research nexus. We also point to the more general strategies heads can use to give effective leadership to a department (see in particular Ramsden, 1998; Blackmore, Gibbs and Shrives, 1999), and how departments can support effective implementation and formulation of the institutional strategies developed in the previous chapter. We recognize that in particular institutions, strategies that we have discussed in the previous chapter for institutional consideration may be more relevant to departmental policies. The more generally departmental focused strategies developed in this chapter are listed below.

DEPARTMENTAL STRATEGIES TO ENHANCE THE TEACHING–RESEARCH NEXUS

- Strategy 1: Develop disciplinary (and departmental) understanding of teaching and research relations.

- Strategy 2: Make it a central consideration in hiring new staff.

- Strategy 3: Ensure it is fostered through how staff roles are defined.

- Strategy 4: Ensure it is fostered through policies for appraisal and staff development.

- Strategy 5: Develop effective synergies between research centres, course planning teams and postgraduate and undergraduate teaching.

- Strategy 6: Audit and review department based courses, structures and policies.

- Strategy 7: Implement university-wide course requirements in ways that reflect department and disciplinary strengths and values.

- Strategy 8: Develop special programmes or structures to foster the nexus.

- Strategy 9: Pay attention to issues of departmental culture.

- Strategy 10: Develop effective synergies between teaching and research strategies.

- Strategy 11: Participate in national (and international) programmes.

STRATEGY 1: DEVELOP DISCIPLINARY (AND DEPARTMENTAL) UNDERSTANDING

Given the central role of the department in organizing staff and other resources, and that it is often here where discipline based groups are housed, it is important for staff to have a clear scholarly understanding of the literature on teaching–research relations so as to inform departmental policies and their practice. Thus, many of the procedures to foster that awareness detailed in chapter 5 (in particular 'organizing events using Boyer/Carnegie analysis etc') may have a greater immediate salience at departmental level. Departments may want to use (part of) departmental meetings, away days or research seminars to develop a (shared) understanding of the generic and discipline based scholarly and research based literature on teaching–research relations.

While one of the great strengths of institutional events is the sharing of experience across very different disciplines, one of the potentially great strengths of considering teaching–research relations at departmental level is that here the focus can be solidly based on disciplinary allegiances. (Healey and Jenkins, in press; Neumann, Parry and Becher, 2002; Rust, 2000). The discipline focus at department level is potentially so important because:

- Department and discipline level is where most courses are planned and resourced and where research is organized in the context of institutional policies.

- Staff may be interested in developing the nexus by seeing examples of effective practice at ensuring teaching–research links as applied to their discipline, drawing on examples and contacts at national and international levels (chapter 7).

- If the research evidence (see chapter 2) does point to the salience of certain disciplinary differences in relations between pedagogy, teaching and research, then there are particular disciplinary issues that have to be resolved (see later discussion in this chapter of student access to research laboratories in science courses). Further examples of a disciplinary pedagogy may lie in the extent to which problem based learning, which offers particularly strong enquiry based pedagogic strategies (Savin-Baden, 2000) is particularly developed in certain professional areas including medicine and engineering.

- Even if the disciplinary pedagogic distinctiveness of the disciplines is to be questioned (Gibbs, 2000), that still leaves the disciplines as central networks of ideas and connections of people; and through such networks, knowledge and beliefs on effective practice are communicated.

STRATEGY 2: MAKE IT A CENTRAL CONSIDERATION IN HIRING NEW STAFF

The key resource that departments can use to secure the nexus is the skills, knowledge and dispositions of the academic staff they select. Therefore, their (potential) dispositions towards linking teaching and research need to be central when hiring new academic staff. Given the mature age structure in many state systems and institutions, this is an issue of pressing importance. Thus, at the University of British Columbia (2000a: 4), discussions of realizing the institutional mission towards teaching and research linkages recognize that 'by the year 2005, over 45 per cent of our faculty will retire'.

We recognize that for some academic positions and in particular institutions, the desire to link or integrate teaching and research will not be the central concern. Clearly, in some circumstances, research or teaching focused staff may be what is required. But for those institutions and departments seeking to integrate teaching and research, this concern needs to be central to the selection process. Ways to achieve this include:

- Ensuring that the promotional literature and job description sent to potential applicants makes clear that the nexus is central to the institutional and departmental mission.

- Use selection procedures that explore this issue, by requiring applicants to give colloquia to staff (and students) on how they intend to construct a course in a way that promotes the nexus.

- For appointments of 'established staff', that is, staff who have some experience of designing courses, one could also require or encourage them to submit a portfolio of evidence of how they have linked teaching and research in their courses so far and strategies they wish to pursue to further develop the nexus.

These procedures may be particularly important in departments at research elite universities, for they may well want to set the nexus as central to their department teaching strategy and culture. But they may also be particularly important outside the research elite. Nelson (2000), a Dean at La Crosse, Wisconsin, points out that this can be a way of attracting to departments at non-elite institutions, high quality young academics who are strongly motivated by research interests and who want to ensure that their career offers potential for pursuing those interests (see discussion of staff motivations in chapter 3).

STRATEGY 3: ENSURE IT IS FOSTERED THROUGH HOW STAFF ROLES ARE DEFINED

Many institutions are moving to more closely define faculty roles and workloads, in part because of the demands for external accountability, but also in recognition (or perhaps belief) that different members of staff have skills and motivations for different roles (see chapter 3). Some would also argue that higher education institutions would be more effective if they moved to much more specially defined staff roles, while ensuring that this is supported by tenure and promotion procedures that effectively value those staff who then concentrate on teaching, advising students, or developing learning materials and so on. In effect such a view is a recognition that in many institutions and departments the teaching and research nexus has collapsed at the level of the individual academic, but still leaves open the possibility of reshaping it at the levels of the student experience and departmental organization (see chapter 2).

We recognize both the logic and the potential gains to individual staff and institutions in such an approach. (Krahenbuhl, 1998; Learey and Williams, 1988; Downey, Coffman and Dyer, 2000). However, moves to specify roles and workloads also threaten the effective integration of teaching and research. The evident danger is that departments will create, in effect, separate categories of research only, or teaching only staff, with some staff whose (limited) teaching is entirely at postgraduate level (with much of their teaching being research supervision re their research areas), while other staff teach many first year students and have effectively no time for research or even scholarship.

This concern has been strongly voiced by some teachers of English and rhetoric in the United States where much of the student or institutional demand is for year one teaching of English composition. These courses are often taught by untenured or part-time staff, yet the rewards for promotion and research opportunities go to those select full time staff who are English literature specialists. Evans (1998) perceives similar (disciplinary) contrasts in the UK in the teaching of foreign languages. Sidaway's (1997: 492) sociological analysis of trends in power and work relations in British geography departments in the 1990s revealed an intensification of staff roles, as illustrated in this comment, 'We are probably going to see in this department a quite definite demarcation between research and teaching and administration.'

To anticipate the next chapter on national policies, in the UK, the Research Assessment Exercise and related pressures, is resulting in:

In some institutions the increasing use of teaching only appointments ... and who may be placed on contracts which mean that the staff

concerned do not have to be entered for the RAE. However the extensive use of this practice... would clearly undermine any claim that research was a prerequisite for high-level teaching.
(JM Port and Associates, 2000: 15)

To which we would add that such practices also question the effective linkage between teaching and research in those departments, unless special measures are taken to ensure that even though the linkage is not always apparent at the level of the individual academic, the linkage is strong in other ways.

Recognizing that many departments worldwide will operate some system of specialist roles and defined workloads, we suggest the following guidelines about workload planning and other matters, for departments that wish to ensure that, at the levels of the student experience, at department and course team levels, and to a lesser extent, at the individual faculty level, the nexus between teaching and research is supported. This pulls us back to the research evidence reviewed in chapter 2 as to at what level we see the nexus, both in theory and to be developed in policy and practice. The guidelines are:

- Ensure that your policies are firmly based on the research evidence on teaching–research relations, workload planning and staff roles. We suspect that too often institutions implement these policies in blissful ignorance of the research evidence. This is not evidence or research based teaching!

- Pay particular attention to the research by Colbeck (1998) on how staff spend their time and roles are allocated and defined (see also chapter 2). Her review of the work on how staff spend their time and how institutions allocate workloads criticizes these studies and related institutional and department policies, for assuming that 'faculty work roles are always fragmented. Faculty workload studies... ask faculty to estimate the time they allocate to teaching, research and service and administrative goals separately' (p 648). However, her own detailed empirical study (and related review of the literature) led her to conclude that 'on average, the faculty observed for this study accomplished teaching and research goals simultaneously during one-fifth of their work-time' (p 664), and that 'increases in faculty productivity may be more likely to occur when working conditions are fostered that encourage the integration of teaching and research'. Her study also showed that '*the broader the definition of what counts as research, the more faculty are able to integrate research and classroom orientated teaching*' (our emphasis). Thus, where staff could count producing textbooks and computing software and other (high level) student learning materials as research, this better enabled them to experience teaching and research as integrated activities.

Also, it seems logical (though we know of no research evidence) that in those departments where (discipline based) pedagogic research and involvement in (national) curriculum development projects are valued in workload allocations (and research funding and sabbaticals and so on), these staff would experience teaching and research activities 'merging in a seamless blend' (Clark, 1987: 70). Huber's (2001: 23)) account of how four Carnegie Scholars had pursued strong scholarly teaching careers revealed both support and tensions in how their departments had viewed their interests, but for these teacher-scholars, balance 'is less about the relationships among different kinds of work and more about their integration'.

- Colbeck (1998: 663) further concluded that: 'the more faculty are involved in department decisions over teaching assignments, the more able they are to integrate teaching and research by teaching courses about their current research topics or incorporating information about their current research in existing required courses.'

- Ensure that certain overarching objectives are set which workload planning has to support: for example, to 'progress and support the effective institutional and department strategy to link teaching and research'.

- As a department, discuss and decide at what level the nexus is to be established and then allocate roles and workloads accordingly. Is the nexus to be achieved at the level of the individual academic, the course team, and/or the department? Or perhaps the focus of integration is not in the academics *per se*, but in student learning, and the department organizes staff roles and the curriculum to ensure that the linkage is achieved at this level.

- Where a department moves to a clear differentiation of roles, special attention is paid to ensuring that effective integration occurs at the level of the student and to ensuring that the department award structure (sabbaticals, promotions and so on) values the different roles and how they contribute to that linkage (see later discussion). Here the research evidence that Fairweather (1993) reports from the United States serves a clear warning. In all institutional types, except the liberal arts colleges, the more time faculty spend on teaching, the lower their pay.

- Consider how the roles and job descriptions of support staff (for example, laboratory technicians, departmental librarians and IT support staff) can support the integration between teaching and research at the level of the department. For example, ensuring that laboratory technicians are trained to support students learning research methods and procedures. This role is also supported by enabling these support staff to be involved in research and scholarly activity.

- Consider placing limits on staff involvement in teaching and /or research. For example, in the previous chapter we noted that at the University of Auckland, staff roles concerning teaching and research were set at any one time within the proportions of 20 per cent teaching to 80 per cent research, and 80 per cent teaching to 20 percent research. These limits are a strategy to better ensure the effective linkage between teaching and research from the level of the individual academic to that of the overall institutional strategy.

- Recognize and support, as does the University of British Columbia Academic Plan (2000b: 5), 'that at different times in their careers, faculty may place different emphases on teaching, research, service, administration or community work'. But such differences in role allocation need to be designed to support the teaching–research nexus at the level(s) the department and institution has decided upon.

- Relatedly, in developing policies and practices, consider the argument by Kreber and Cranton (2000: 217) (based, they argue, on research evidence in cognitive and developmental psychology), 'that faculty should be advised to focus on either research or teaching at different times during the early years and that integration of professorial roles should be expected at later stages'. They argue that a key role for selected senior staff in a department is to act as mentors to junior faculty advising them on how to develop integrated roles.

- Pay special attention to the roles and needs of part-time and untenured staff. Around the world HE institutions are now characterized by the (increased) use of part-time and untenured staff. In developing a teaching–research nexus, departments need at worst to ensure that part-time and untenured staff are not just used for low level teaching and freeing up certain full time staff to concentrate on research. At best, part-time and untenured staff should be supported in scholarly and research activity and in helping to ensure that at the level of the student experience there is an effective teaching–research nexus.

STRATEGY 4: ENSURE IT IS FOSTERED THROUGH POLICIES FOR APPRAISAL AND STAFF DEVELOPMENT

The department is generally where appraisal and staff development is most immediately implemented. Institutional policies can ensure a general framework that supports teaching–research integration, for instance, by ensuring that certain key issues are covered in appraisal documents and that strategies for staff development have to define and evaluate how the teaching–research nexus is being developed. The department can ensure these general strategies are delivered and tailored to the particular departmental strategies and disciplinary concerns.

STRATEGY 5: DEVELOP EFFECTIVE SYNERGIES BETWEEN RESEARCH CENTRES, COURSE PLANNING TEAMS AND POSTGRADUATE AND UNDERGRADUATE TEACHING

In an analysis of the impact of the UK Research Assessment Exercises in 1992 and 1996, McNay concluded that the RAE had contributed within some institutions and departments to:

> Structural changes: research centres housed staff freed from teaching responsibilities; graduate schools became the arenas for research, leaving departments to organize undergraduate teaching. Each of these (developments) was particular and peculiar, *but the trend was gradually of a separation, structurally of research from teaching*.
> (McNay, 1999: 196; our emphasis added)

Similar tensions are apparent in other state systems, including some of the US graduate schools which are clearly research focused and structurally separate from undergraduate teaching, and where some specialist researchers have little or no contact with students except for doctoral level supervision. Again, that may be effective in certain ways and contexts; but in terms of our agenda it is a negative model, for it separates teaching from research in multiple ways. In setting out some positive models and suggested practices, readers are warned that these come mainly from informal observation and discussions with colleagues. There is little or no research to guide us and few published studies of how departments organize themselves to manage and support the teaching–research nexus. One such published study: that does suggest some general principles is the School of Humanities at Oxford Brookes set out in the boxed case study.

A SCHOOL STRATEGY TO LINK TEACHING AND RESEARCH

The School of Humanities at Oxford Brookes (UK) (a former polytechnic, until recently only funded nationally for teaching), a department which had few research active staff, was declining in staff numbers and effectively only did undergraduate teaching (in art history, English and history). Its position in the institution was marginal and threatened (Perkins, 1998). Over 10 years it transformed itself, in part around an explicit strategy of linking teaching and research, developing a strong research culture and bringing in external research income. Specifically:

- A high level researcher/reader was appointed to support colleagues in all three disciplines to undertake research.

- This research strategy paid off in terms of grades in the 1992, 1996 and 2001 RAEs and in bids for external funding for research.

- A range of interdisciplinary and discipline based postgraduate courses was initiated. These required extra work from staff in preparation and delivery. These courses, or rather their students, also brought the fees to hire more staff.

- Where possible extra staffing resources went to hiring full time staff who were teachers and researchers, and not on hiring specialist researchers, as well as limiting the use of part-time teaching staff.

- 'Non-active' researchers were supported in teaching specialist courses at postgraduate level on particular areas of interest, and this in turn led to them publishing in these areas.

- The stimulus of graduate supervision and postgraduate teaching gave an intellectual vitality to the School, which was then apparent in the revision of the undergraduate programme.

Clearly readers should be suspicious of this account, partly because it comes from the institution where we work. As does the school, we have an interest in painting it in 'happy colours'. There is however a dark side to the story. As one of the staff puts it: 'YES... BUT the result is that many of us are overstretched. Achievement is high but so too are stress levels; people are working longer hours. The words "undergraduate teaching" feature far less in School Board agendas than they used to (and are) displaced by phrases such as research income and MA funds' (Pope, 1998: 5). However, the context here is also national underfunding and continued cuts in higher education, and the structural separation of external research and teaching 'assessment' (see chapter 7).

The case study and our related discussions with colleagues in a range of disciplines and institutions do point to ways departments can seek to organize research centres, and undergraduate and postgraduate teaching. Here are some suggested strategies:

- Use research centres to provide the links between staff with cognate research interests and to make effective bids for external funds, including bids to develop pedagogy and curricular materials from these research studies.

- Consider ensuring that these research centres or units take a lead role or a role in undergraduate and postgraduate teaching. Such a role might involve ensuring that the courses are soundly based on current research in the discipline. This might include making some (upper level undergraduate) courses the responsibility of research teams. This means that aspects of the organization of teaching can support research. Research led teaching teams can then readily arrange between themselves times for individuals to go on sabbaticals, attend conferences and prepare curricular materials without undue disruption of teaching.

- Appoint staff to these research teams with particular interests and expertise in developing curricula and curricula materials and textbooks or e-learning resources that draw extensively on that research.

- Recognize that there may be important disciplinary differences in organizing and linking teaching and research around research teams. Thus, in a discussion of linking teaching and research in the particular context of graduate student supervision, Kyvik and Smeby argue that:

  Such arrangements need to take variations and knowledge structures and research organization into consideration. Research traditions in the humanities and, to some extent, the social sciences, are individually orientated. In contrast to the natural and medical sciences and technology, there seems less to be gained from collaboration in research. To get access to resources and expensive technical equipment scientists have to co-operate. (Kyvik and Smeby, 1994: 236)

- On this point also see Smeby (2002). Perhaps, then, the challenge here is for humanities departments among others to consider how science research and science departments are organized, and how that can be transferred effectively to their disciplinary practices. For example, we saw in chapter 4 how arts and humanities staff at the University of

Michigan, working with community groups, have involved students in a range of long-term staff-led research projects, within which individual students can develop a research project that is limited in both duration and timing (Scobey, 2002).

- Consider how staff research seminars can be selectively, made available to undergraduates as in the case study of Nottingham Trent.

CASE STUDY: HISTORY AT NOTTINGHAM TRENT

The Forward Research Group in the history department at Nottingham Trent (UK) (again a former polytechnic that was originally not funded for research) initiated a series of research seminars for staff and postgraduates with linked research interests (Currie, 2000). This was clearly aimed at developing a staff research culture.

One feature of this seminar series was a discussion of draft writings by staff and postgraduates in these research areas. From this other changes followed:

- This research culture initiated a series of new modules for year 1 and year 2 undergraduates. The assignments in these modules are a piece of work that matches staff research interests.

- Students on these modules were encouraged to attend selected talks by outside speakers.

- This led to some of these undergraduate students choosing to attend some of the sessions on draft publications and in turn, seeing this as an opportunity to discuss their draft undergraduate dissertation writings.

- This dissertation element has become a formalized part of the seminar series, and the modern languages department has adapted the overall 'Forward' model.

This set of processes and procedures has become for this department a central way it develops a discipline and departmental approach to linking teaching and research.

- Consider how resources, including expensive technical equipment, that support staff research can also be used selectively to support post-graduate and undergraduate teaching. Thus, a UK science department preparing for an external teaching quality assessment was challenged by one member of its staff as to how it was delivering the statement in the required self-assessment document portraying the department as one where 'teaching and research were intimately linked'. (The department and the institution are anonymous!) The ensuing discussion led to the realization that many of the department's laboratories were controlled by research active staff who did little or no undergraduate teaching and, in particular, were not involved in supervising undergraduate dissertations, which is where the department's teaching strategy document emphasized the close connection between teaching and research! Immediately these staff were reassigned, as were their laboratories, to support undergraduate dissertations. Of course we should also ask what happened after the teaching quality assessment visit! Although this is a particular case study, the principles of departments reviewing how research resources can support (undergraduate) teaching can be generally applied.

- Consider how the raw data and results of staff research can be incorporated into courses: for example, undergraduate research training courses can reinterpret data gathered by staff for research projects, or can be part of ongoing departmental research and/or consultancy projects. Here, the support or the central involvement of department and institutional librarians and IT specialists can be central to developing resources that foster effective linkages between resources for research and for teaching.

- Consider how postgraduate students, and their research interests and expertise, can be used to support undergraduate students to see connections between teaching and research and for selected undergraduates to see themselves as future postgraduates and researchers.

- Consider also how postgraduate students are supported to see that any future career in academia offers opportunities to link their roles as teachers and researchers. This issue was of course addressed in the discussion of institutional policies in chapter 6, but there are more specific strategies that departments can use to develop the nexus through postgraduates. See the case study of textbook writing that follows.

LINKING TEACHING AND RESEARCH FOR POSTGRADUATES THROUGH TEXTBOOK WRITING

At Michigan and Colorado Universities, staff in the sociology departments have formally involved postgraduate students in the writing of staff authored textbooks through various optional course work assignments (Zinn and Eitzen, 2000).

- Postgraduate students (often based on their own research) have been involved in textbook writing, through written boxed inserts, being co-authors of chapters, and writing manuals and assessment items including 'objective' test banks.

- As well as aiding their future employability (and immediate income), this is explicitly directed to Boyer's (1990) critiques of graduate schools solely focusing on discovery research. For it is claimed that these textbook activities support postgraduate students' understanding and valuing of integrative scholarship; and it 'should make prospective teachers become better educators as they think about pedagogy, search for appropriate audio-visual aids, and consider various forms of testing and evaluation' (Zinn and Eitzen, 2000: 366).

STRATEGY 6: AUDIT AND REVIEW DEPARTMENT BASED COURSES, STRUCTURES AND POLICIES

In the introduction to this chapter we emphasized that in many institutions resources, including staff time, are organized at departmental level. In relation to this, in many institutions, departments play a central role in determining, resourcing and reviewing the courses that students experience, albeit under procedures defined at institutional level. One possible strategy for a department wishing to strengthen the teaching–research nexus is systematically to review or audit the current range of courses in terms of how they support (or hinder) the nexus. In the box are questions that departments can ask themselves (and/or that institutions can ask of them!) to audit their courses and structures. They were developed in 2002 by Roger Zetter, acting Head of Planning at Oxford Brookes, following focus groups by staff on their perceptions of teaching–research relations in four UK institutions (Zetter, 2002). A strong theme of this focus group research was the importance of departmental structures in either supporting or hindering the nexus (see discussion of project Link in chapter 7). Then having completed the review, decide on and implement measures to strengthen the nexus. This is demonstrated in the following case study of health care.

QUESTIONS FOR A DEPARTMENT AUDIT

- How does the learning and teaching strategy articulate research and teaching and learning links? (And how does the research strategy articulate such links?)

- How are the teaching and research cultures organized, motivated and resourced? Are they managed for mutual engagement?

  - How do research teams and course teaching teams link with each other? How are these links facilitated?

  - Are research 'clusters' also 'teaching teams'?

- How are teaching staff 'managed' in developing research capacity and vice versa?

Developing an inclusive culture

- What are the mechanisms for disseminating and communicating research outputs and teaching practice? Are they shared?

- How is the research culture and activity given visibility to students? How do they come into contact with departmental research?

- What are the strategies to disseminate research based teaching experience from the module level?

- What profile is given to pedagogic research? How is it applied?

Case study: developing research-based education in health care

The School of Health Care Studies at Oxford Brookes undertook a comprehensive review of all its courses (and associated staffing) to strengthen how students: a) understood health care practice as evidence-based; b) could themselves understand the nature of, and to an extent carry out, research; c) could ensure that students were informed consumers of research in the way that they practised professionally, through developing in students skills in critical appraisal and research skills in interpreting and applying knowledge based on research evidence.

Pressures causing this review included:

- The growing national and international professional requirements for staff who can carry out evidence based health care, and the related demands by postgraduate and post experience students seeking such professional qualifications. (This is analogous to the view that teaching should be based on research evidence on how students learn, outlined in chapter 1.)

- Student evaluations, combined with comments from external examiners and lecturers, indicating some difficulties in how students in the school experienced and perceived the research based elements of their courses.

- The lack of clear specification of the research skills needed at each programme level, and awareness that some of the assessment strategies in courses did not support the effective development of these skills (see chapter 4).

Strategies to strengthen the nexus included:

- 'Establishment in January 2000 of a Research Education Steering Group to inform a proactive and strategic approach to the implementation of a spiral curriculum for research education (and evidence-based practice) across pre-registration, post qualifying and postgraduate programmes in the School' (Appleton, 2000: 4; Appleton and Sanders, 2000).

- Appointment of a new member of academic staff as Principal Lecturer in Research Education, to take a central role in auditing practice and developing policy.

- Review and, where necessary, revision of all courses in terms of their current practice in evidence based health care, with particular attention to reviewing their current learning outcomes and related assessment strategies and a 'research skills audit' of all courses in terms of whether particular research skills were taught, practised and assessed in particular modules. In many cases such revisions were to make more explicit what had previously been implicit.

- Requirement that all field and course teams develop a strand of education for evidence based practice through all programmes.

- Developing a common dissertation requirement and specification for all multi-professional programmes.

- Staff training and support to develop a core of staff with expertise in research education to teach the research 'training' courses and lead in the supervision of student dissertations.

- With the above tasks completed, the Steering Group from September 2001 is to focus on monitoring practice and policy.

**STRATEGY 7: IMPLEMENT UNIVERSITY-WIDE COURSE
REQUIREMENTS IN WAYS THAT REFLECT DEPARTMENT AND
DISCIPLINARY STRENGTHS AND VALUES**

As we saw in chapter 5, some institutions are now developing university-wide requirements for courses that seek to integrate teaching and research. To be effective, such requirements need to be implemented by departments in ways that reflect their particular strengths, structures, staffing, and disciplinary conceptions of both teaching and research, as for example the case study of evidence based health care above. The case study of Royal Roads is a powerful example of this general principle.

**Applied environmental science and business entrepreneurial projects
at Royal Roads University:
(http://www.royalroads.ca/ste/bsces/student_projects.htm)**

Royal Roads (http://www.royalroads.ca/) in British Columbia, Canada is a public university focused on the needs of working professionals. All programmes have a strong focus on linking theory and practice, are competency based and have undergraduate graduation requirements for carrying out a team based original research investigation. The Royal Roads University research model focuses primarily on an applied action orientated, problem orientated, problem solving response to market needs. These university-wide values and requirements with respect to these major research projects are implemented at department level in accordance with disciplinary concerns, as shown in the two mini case studies of environmental science and entrepreneurial management (Paget *et al*, 2001).

Environmental science
The BSc in Environmental Science programme at Royal Roads University is an intensive, 12-month one that is equivalent to the final two years of a four-year undergraduate degree. The degree has a strong focus on students carrying out applied research projects in line with the values and philosophy of the programme and university (sustainability, leadership, conflict resolution and entrepreneurship). All learners in the BSc in Environmental Science engage in an original team based research project as part of their degree requirements. The particular features of the environmental science major project are:

- The projects are carried out during the final eight months of the degree, concurrently with other courses.

- The major project is the central component that integrates previous course based knowledge and demonstrates the program competencies in environmental science and other required outcomes such as teamwork and communication skills.

- Projects are problem based and authentic. They involve students working with a community group, private company, government agency, or in a partnership between two or three of these parties on an issue relating to ecological sustainability.

- Students are assigned to work teams of four to six, and the teams are determined by staff to ensure that student teams have a variety of personalities and skills.

- Groups then consider the projects that have been proposed for investigation by various clients and prepare a bid to work on a particular project, much like a consulting company proposal to a prospective client.

- The bid outlines project milestones, specified outputs, budget, qualifications of the team, and research methodology.

- Recent projects include: community stewardship initiatives for a local lake, improved groundwater treatment for a local environmental action group, and a study of the effects of cleaning solvents on the sewage treatment system performance of British Columbia Ferries.

Entrepreneurial management
Students in the entrepreneurial management programme at Royal Roads are similarly required to pass a major research project but, as with the environmental science programme, the particular requirements of the entrepreneurial project reflects both university and discipline based values. Its particular features include:

- The overall objective to 'expose learners to the process of conceptualising a new venture through the development and presentation of a plan for a business that is financially feasible and ready to launch'.

- The project is first and foremost an academic exercise executed in teams of five learners.

- Each of the learner teams is expected to develop a comprehensive business plan by applying and integrating all of the subject areas in the programme (marketing, people at work, finance, accounting, communications, sustainable development and so on).

- The research and the resulting business plan should not only pass a real-world test of financial viability but also should be able to be used as an operational plan for management to execute the entire vision of the venture for at least the first three years.

- The project is completed in four progressive phases over a five-month period.

- At each phase in the process, learner teams present their analyses of the business opportunity and the plan to exploit it in written format to External Entrepreneurial Advisors (EEAs) who are assigned to each team. The learner teams deliver oral presentations in phases 2, 3 and 4 to the EEAs and a panel of seasoned entrepreneurs, bankers and other industry experts for feedback.

- The EEA has primary responsibility for the assessment of the project, which is a mixture of individual and team based assessment.

- Recent projects include companies developing new roofing materials, biomass refinery technology, and a company developing fitness centres in airports.

STRATEGY 8: DEVELOP SPECIAL PROGRAMMES OR STRUCTURES TO FOSTER THE NEXUS

In chapter 5 we showed how institutions could develop the nexus through institution-wide programmes often aimed at selected well motivated students, as demonstrated in the case study of Rutgers University. Such a strategy can of course also be developed at departmental level, and does not necessarily depend on institutional requirements. Such department based programmes can be clearly discipline based, in both curriculum and pedagogy, as with the following case study from biology. Or as with the Gemstone project described below, special programmes can be initiated in an individual discipline or department, but then reach out to other disciplines or departments. These discipline based approaches may be particularly of interest to outside donors, because of the congruence between the programme concerns and donor interests.

Undergraduate biology research program (UBRP) at the University of Arizona, Tucson

Research 1 universities can offer students a science education in their laboratories that is available nowhere else.
(Bender, Ward and Wells, 1994: 133)

In chapter 5 we reported on how selected research based universities seek to demonstrate the added value undergraduate students can obtain from studying there in exchange for higher fees. Such institutional policies need to be complemented, or maybe initiated, at department level. One example of such a department based initiative is the UBRP at Tucson (Bender, Ward and Wells, 1994; Bender, 1999). The central features of the programme include:

- The philosophy that 'the best way a research university can enhance undergraduate science education is *to maximize undergraduate access to research laboratories'* (Bender, Ward and Wells, 1994: 12, emphasis added).

- The focus is in part to attract able undergraduate students to consider a research career through graduate school or enter allied fields such as medicine.

- Students work with faculty to carry out research projects. Beginning in 1988 with 19 students working with 13 faculty, in 2000 it supported 140 students who could choose to work with more than 250 faculty.

- Much of the funding is through external grants, in particular, from the Howard Hughes Medical Institute and the National Science Foundation (see chapter 7 on national policies). 'External funding was necessary to sustain this effort' (Bender, 1999: 118).

- Staff are selected partly on the basis of commitment to the program but also through having been successful in obtaining an external grant that helps pay participating students a wage for their research work.

- Paying students is, in part, to better ensure that able, committed students do not have to seek other paid work to support their studies.

- There is a full time program, a director and staff and student advisory committee.

- Students are selected, in part, on grades in science and mathematics and on a statement of interest. (They do not have to produce a research proposal.) 'Student applicants are self-selected because they already are seeking an independent research experience and thus tend to be the more dedicated students' (Bender, 1994: 131). This is one illustration of the evidence about student motivation discussed in chapter 3.

- Once selected for the program, students interview several faculty with research money or research areas, and select the best match for their interests.

- There is a strong commitment, and programme funding to support women and minority student access to the programme.

- The program starts early in the student's undergraduate programme: for many in the summer preceding the student's second year. 'We learned that a period of full time effort is necessary for students to acquire enough expertise to do independent research' (Bender, Ward and Wells, 1994: 131). 'Once accepted on the program, students can continue in the program, working (part-time) year round until they graduate' (Bender, 1999: 120). 'Students work full-time for 12 weeks in the summer and roughly 20 hours per week during the academic year' (Bender, Ward and Wells, 1994: 131).

- There is an annual conference at which students present their methodology and findings through a poster. They are then encouraged to submit their research to external conferences, and successful applicants obtain travel and conference fees. Many then have their research published, often with the supporting faculty as co- or lead author(s).

- Clearly this is a selective programme. The thinking behind it and many of the staff centrally involved have also spawned a radical revision to introductory courses for mainstream students. Thus, a two semester year one course emphasizes experimental approaches to biology: and this has led to increased enrolments, and gives initial exposure to research methodologies for those few students who select and are selected to UBRP.

The Maryland Gemstone Program (http://www.gemstone.umd.edu/)

The Gemstone Program is a four-year undergraduate degree programme for honours students that was initiated in 1994 at the University of Maryland. Students also complete their major in engineering, business and so on.

- It was conceived and developed by the then Dean of Engineering, and is organized through the Institute for Systems Research, a cross-disciplinary research and education institute within the School of Engineering.

- The central focus is on students working in teams, researching and attempting to solve a specific issue that addresses technological, ethical, and social and business elements: for example, developing an effective and cost-efficient global positioning driven bus-scheduling system.

- The engineering base is clearly still there, but students majoring in business, social science and business and humanities are sought for the program.

- The program has about 700 students focused on over 50 projects.

- Undergraduates from a range of majors are teamed together in groups of 10–15 students, with a faculty mentor.

- In a first-year curriculum that focuses on research design, team working and contemporary societal and technological issues, students also develop a research theme or research question.

- The culmination of the four-year project is a book length team thesis completed in the senior year.

- The senior year also contains a research conference where each team gives a preliminary, critiqued presentation.

STRATEGY 9: PAY ATTENTION TO ISSUES OF DEPARTMENTAL CULTURE

The generic pedagogic literature draws attention to the importance of the departmental culture (Parlett, 1977) and, relatedly, to the 'hidden curriculum' (Snyder, 1971), those informal messages and values that students and staff pick up and experience. We suspect that in terms of departmental policies to promote teaching and research integration, staff perceptions and experience of the departmental culture may be particularly important to what 'down the line' students experience. If staff pick up the clues that research publications, or ensuring that courses delivering transferable or key skills, are what mainly count, then teaching and research are likely to be seen as separate areas, and only one side of the potential nexus is valued.

One way to take this issue forward is to consider how an anthropologist would analyse your departmental culture. If he or she sat in on Departmental Boards and informal staff meetings, how would your departmental culture be described in terms of the 'hidden curriculum' of teaching–research relations? What then are the messages for your departmental policies and procedures?

**STRATEGY 10: DEVELOP EFFECTIVE SYNERGIES BETWEEN
TEACHING AND RESEARCH STRATEGIES**

Explicit to the above discussion is the perspective that the link needs to be
developed through a range of strategies that seek to maximize the beneficial synergies between teaching and research. Certainly in the UK, most if
not all departments have a research strategy; the requirements and the
rewards of the Research Assessment Exercise have stimulated, indeed,
required a strategic approach to research. Also, the requirements of the
external review of teaching and experience in developing institutional
teaching strategies have caused some departments to develop teaching
strategies. Even if these are not formally written down there are, in effect,
implicit strategies or strategies in action.

In our experience, these strategies for teaching and research are
generally developed in formal isolation from each other. Informally, at
department level there may be implicit links as the same people may be
involved in developing strategies at this level, a situation which is much less
likely to occur at institutional level. Yet, given the central role of departments in enacting the nexus, effective integration between teaching and
research needs to be managed strategically at that level. A recent research
study of UK institutions (and would the results be different elsewhere?)
specifically about departments of history, chemistry, engineering and
business studies revealed:

> If teaching and research are as inseparable as many participants
> claimed, the lack of explicit strategies to promote this synergy is inter-
> esting. The discussions with heads of department and other
> managers of staff time indicated that on a managerial level, it is more
> convenient for teaching and research to be treated as separate activ-
> ities. On an intellectual level, however, academic managers would
> rather perceive the two to be synergistic. What seems to be missing is
> an intellectual perception of teaching and research as integrated. For
> example, *we visited many departments where Research Committees and
> Teaching Committees had been established, but these two bodies worked inde-
> pendently of each other.*
> (Coate, Barnett and Williams, 2001: 162; our emphasis)

**STRATEGY 11: PARTICIPATE IN NATIONAL (AND
INTERNATIONAL) PROGRAMMES**

The department can also assist and support staff (and in some cases
students) to participate in and learn from national and international

organizations that promote and support teaching–research connections, particularly those associated with their discipline.

We have shown that the research evidence cautions us that the teaching–research nexus is not automatic; that central to establishing the nexus is seeing research and teaching as enquiry; that to ensure the nexus requires actions from the level of the individual, the course team, and through the department and institutional levels. We now move up to the levels of national and international organizations and policies and consider how they can support the nexus.

7

Organizing the national and international administration of higher education to link teaching and research

Despite the evidence of a synergistic relationship between teaching and research, we make no recommendation about this: it would be wrong to allow teaching issues to influence the allocation of funds for research.
(HEFCE, 2000b: para 175, 26)

The New Zealand Education Amendment Act of 1990 identified five characteristics of a University, including that at universities 'research and teaching are closely interdependent and most of their teaching is done by people who are active in advancing knowledge'. The Act also states that a 'degree' is a qualification awarded following a course of advanced learning, that is *taught mainly by people engaged in research.*
(Cited in Woodhouse, 1998: 41; emphasis added)

Active research experience is one of the most effective techniques for attracting talented undergraduates to and retaining them in careers in mathematics, science and engineering. Too few such experiences are now available. The Research Experience for Undergraduates program (REU) is designed to help meet this need.
(NSF, 1998: 1)

Teaching benefits from research and scholarly activities; conversely teaching contributes to the development of research. To exploit this synergy, the relationship between teaching and research needs to be actively managed. The opportunity to do research is an important reason why people decide on an academic career.
(HEFCE, 2000a: 4)

The central themes running through this book are five linked perspectives:

- The value judgements of the critical and central role of universities in helping students and society at large to both value and understand knowledge forged through research.

- That for many academic staff their own motivation as teachers is linked to their involvement in discipline based research and scholarship.

- The strong research evidence that the teaching–research linkage is not automatic and indeed in many ways is problematic.

- The growing research evidence that (staff) research can aid student learning and motivate students.

- Then perhaps the central theme that realizing this valued potential teaching–research nexus requires action in a whole variety of ways and levels, and in ways that are congruent with the research evidence and the institutional, department and disciplinary contexts.

The organization of the book reflects the perspective that the 'level of action' is a useful way of conceiving the issues and setting out a range of strategies that can be taken to realize the desired nexus. Having started from a review of the available research evidence, we have considered what individuals and course teams can do, and then looked at the role of academic institutions and departments. As we have moved up the levels we have emphasized that suggested actions are often not as well grounded on the research evidence as we think is needed. In making suggestions for academics and policy makers we hope that in earlier chapters we have been sensitive to disciplinary and institutional variations. Such sensitivity is perhaps even more important as we turn to the national (and international) levels. For national higher education systems vary greatly in culture, purpose, organization and funding arrangements. We are well aware that one cannot take one element from a national system, and simply transplant it elsewhere. We also recognize that our thinking is strongly shaped by working in the British system, which is a national, centrally directed system and very different from, say, the more diverse and more privately funded US system. Clearly our perspective is also shaped by working in a national culture that has both valued the teaching–research nexus and in recent years challenged that link. Perhaps at times the spectre of the UK Research Assessment Exercise does hang over this chapter.

However, we have sought through reading and research visits to ensure a more international perspective to this and other chapters. We have also benefited from e-mail contacts with many colleagues internationally, and the Web sites that now make more international perspective so readily possible. No doubt our thinking reflects our national and institutional backgrounds. So in particular in this chapter we ask that readers interpret and assess the validity and value of the strategies we develop next against their own national (and institutional and professional or disciplinary) contexts. While in seeking to ensure a more international focus to this work we recognize that international here largely means the UK, North America and Australasia. That's a very limited international perspective!

REASONS FOR FOCUSING AT NATIONAL AND INTERNATIONAL LEVELS

We see at the national level, and perhaps increasingly the international level, the vital importance in realizing the teaching and research nexus. The reasons for focusing at the national and international levels include:

- Governments take a central role in determining the funding for universities both directly and through policies for student support and taxation etc.

- In some state systems, governments take a very proactive and direct role in determining the organization of and purposes of universities, both for teaching and for research; and also in reviewing how universities are meeting national needs. The key role of governments towards the nexus is further developed in the next section.

- In state systems, such as the United States, where the central government's roles are more limited than in centralized states, other national agencies, including quasi state organizations such as the US regional accrediting organizations and private donors such as the Carnegie Association and the Pew Foundation take on roles that elsewhere would be directly organized and funded through the formal state.

- Universities at national, and increasingly at international level, are making strategic alliances with cognate universities in moves in part designed to differentiate themselves from local competitors. Clearly for some institutions (and not just the research elite), one of the main considerations in setting up such national/international links is in terms of institutional missions towards teaching and research.

- Academic ideas and innovations are developed and fostered through disciplines and interdisciplines, and these ideas flow nationally and internationally. Harnessing staff motivations to realize the nexus involves thinking how national and international disciplinary associations can support the nexus.

- The linked processes of globalization and information and communications technology are changing the classic connections of academics as teacher/researchers working with students at fixed locations. In supporting the nexus we have to consider how we recognize and work with such processes (Newby, 1999; Marginson, 2000).

Given the key role of governments we start by further developing why we see their roles as so central to realizing the nexus: and then turn to more specific and not necessarily government based strategies that can be developed at national and international levels.

THE ROLE OF GOVERNMENTS, THE NATIONAL ECONOMY AND THE NEXUS

The role of governments in shaping teaching and research is perhaps becoming more important for two broadly different reasons: issues of meaning and purpose, and issues of funding. Many state systems are trying to work out the role of universities (and their roles towards teaching and research) in the context of a mass higher education system where 30 to 50 per cent of an age cohort goes into 'higher' education. Does the traditional Humboldt model of the teacher–researcher and the 'classic connection' (see chapter 2) of the close interdependence of teaching and research still make sense in terms of meeting student needs and that of society (Schimank and Winnes, 2000)? Should we hold on to these traditional connections, or would students and society benefit more from a higher education curriculum where, for example, 'key employability skills' are paramount? This might call for the research elements in the curriculum to be downplayed; a view that is given further weight as governments and other national (and in federal systems, state level) governments consider the cost of funding (staff and student) research. These financial considerations reinforce the arguments for research selectivity. These financial and resource pressures then further call into question what we mean by 'higher education'; and whether that meaning has to recognize varied meanings and interpretations, only some of which focus on the nexus as the central feature of higher education.

Governments now do fund higher education to carry on research which is seen as productive in terms of the economy and answering questions on which government and society requires research evidence to guide national policies. Governments and some university authorities argue (on the basis of research evidence?) that research should be concentrated in particular departments or institutions. Beckhradnia (1998: 3), Director of Policy for the English Funding Council (HEFCE), points out that while in teaching the aim of the Funding Council is to be relatively equitable in funding; in research, 'we take the view that it is in the national interest that we should concentrate the money on units and departments which are of the highest quality.' The result of similar trends in the US postwar was the rise of the large research universities and departments and graduate schools and a highly differentiated higher education system, in which in all disciplines, research and research funding was, and is, highly concentrated (Boyer, 1990).

In some national systems including in continental Europe, for example France, 'teaching and research have been institutionalised in separate social subsystems. (Thus in France) teaching has been the responsibility of the universities and grande ecoles, whereas research was mainly delegated to mission orientated research organizations with their own statutes, budgets, bodies of full time researchers, and recruitment and career patterns' (Schimank and Winnes, 2000: 404). Clearly while there are such research institutes in Australasia, North America and the UK, in those state systems most research is conducted in universities. In the past such research would often have been relatively equitably distributed. However the recent trend has been for governments to create some system of dual or separate support systems for teaching and research: and to concentrate research in selected institutions and departments, and at times to show little or no concern as to how these two functions might be linked. Thus a recent Australian government review of research and research training in higher education sees research in terms of wealth creation, funding is to become more highly selective and competitive to ensure world class research and researchers. Discussion of how to ensure links to under-graduate teaching and learning is conspicuous by its absence (Commonwealth of Australia, 1999). The absence of any concern to ensure the nexus is both acknowledged and implicitly justified in the recent UK review of research.

> Despite the evidence of a synergistic relationship between teaching and research, we make no recommendation about this: it would be wrong to allow teaching issues to influence the allocation of funds for research. (HEFCE, 2000b: para 175, 26)

Such national policies and pressures point to a de-coupling of teaching and research; with research being concentrated in selected institutions, and inside institutions to certain departments and selected staff; and a 'research based curriculum' restricted to the more able or more motivated students, and possibly to those who can pay for this 'added value'.

Yet the perhaps contradictory pressure is that research is now seen as vital to the new 'knowledge economy', with implications for both the curriculum and the organization and funding of research. The emerging economy is seen as one that requires individuals with creativity and ability to create, find and synthesize new knowledge. However in the view of a recent Demos report, 'our educational structures are lagging behind. The dominant educational paradigm still focuses on what students know, rather than how they use that knowledge' (Seltzer and Bentley, 1999: 9). Research itself is being seen in much wider and more contested terms (Brew, 2001a). Furthermore, and particularly important in this context of governments and economic policy, is the view that much knowledge (research) is generated in application, in short as Mode 2 knowledge (Gibbons *et al*, 1994). If these arguments have validity, then students' understanding of the research process and ability to do research may be the vital key skills, and therefore should be central to the curriculum for all or most higher education students; and national systems should ensure that universities deliver that 'research based' (or perhaps a 'research informed') curriculum.

POSSIBLE STRATEGIES FOR NATIONAL AND INTERNATIONAL ORGANIZATIONS

Recognizing both the diversity of national higher education systems and the limited research and scholarly base on which we can draw to suggest actions at those levels, these are the strategies that we think can be developed by national and international organizations to support the nexus. To repeat earlier cautions, this chapter is very much a 'work in progress', with ideas to stimulate others, both policy makers and researchers. In some areas, for example the discussion immediately below on institutional diversity, we comment only briefly on major issues to bring out their relevance to the teaching–research nexus. Possible strategies for national and international organizations are:

- Strategy 1: Build it into the statutory and legal definitions of HE institutions, degree and professional requirements.

- Strategy 2: Ensure there are limited negative impacts from research selectivity.

- Strategy 3: Require research selectivity to support research areas that directly support the nexus.

- Strategy 4: Fund and support all institutions and staff for (discipline based) scholarly activity.

- Strategy 5: Develop external reviews of teaching and research that explicitly support the linkage.

- Strategy 6: National and international disciplinary organizations can support the nexus.

- Strategy 7: Develop national and international organizations and projects to support the nexus.

STRATEGY 1: BUILD IT INTO THE STATUTORY AND LEGAL DEFINITIONS OF HE INSTITUTIONS, DEGREE AND PROFESSIONAL REQUIREMENTS

In many state systems the title of 'university' is a legal statement granted through central government or through some other public agency. Even without such a legal or statutory requirement, all state systems need to decide what distinguishes higher education from further education and corporate training. Yet all state systems seeking to develop a mass higher education system need to develop institutional diversity; to guard against 'mission drift', where the research elite and discipline based 'discovery research' becomes the 'gold standard' to which all aspire (Brown, 1999; Newby 1999).

In that context, particular strategies that state systems could consider include the following.

Build the nexus into statutory definitions of a university
The prime example of this is New Zealand where at present (the system is under review! see later discussion) the Education Amendment Act of 1990 identified five characteristics of a university, including that at universities '*research and teaching are closely interdependent* and most of their teaching is done by people who are active in advancing knowledge'. The Act also states that a 'degree is a qualification awarded following a course of advanced learning, that is *taught mainly by people engaged in research*' (cited in Woodhouse, 1998: 41; emphasis added). Perhaps we are in danger here of diluting such an approach, by suggesting that such a 'definition' might also recognize the importance of public scholarship. Possibly the nexus would be more realistically and thus more effectively delivered by requiring universities and degree granting institutions to ensure the interdependence between student learning and discovery research through integrative scholarship and professional practice.

Build it into any public classifications of universities
Certain state systems recognize institutional diversity through some classification of universities. Probably one of the best examples of this is the US Carnegie classification developed in 1971 originally as a research tool, but

now used by universities and state agencies (including research granting bodies such as the National Science Foundation) to define and differentiate institutional mission and functions. The 1994 classification identified seven categories (for example, Research Universities 1), as having 50 or more doctorates per year, and US$40 million dollars or more per year of research income from outside grants. In terms of developing and encouraging the teaching–research nexus, the limits of this classification include focusing on measuring research grants and research activity and not on measures that encourage the nexus, including measures that capture the student experience (of research). Furthermore, while its original intended purposes included preserving 'and even increasing the diversity of institutions of higher education by type and by program; resisting homogenisation' (cited in McCormick, 2000a), the effect has been to push institutions to move up the 'Carnegie ladder' through increasing measures such as numbers of staff with doctorates. Lee Shulman, the President of the Carnegie Foundation, observes that:

> One of the great strengths of the higher education system in the United States is its diversity of institutions. One pernicious effect of the Carnegie classification from the perspective of the Foundation is the tendency of many institutions to emulate the model of a large research university.
> (Shulman, 2000: 3)

Indeed from our outside perspective the effects *may* include the structural separation of teaching from research, and perhaps contribute to the negative impacts that Astin (1993) and others have found as institutional priorities towards research and cause research to become separate from student learning. (See chapter 2; and also note the parallels with what we see below are the unintended consequences of the UK Research Assessment Exercise.) 'In effect the Classification plays a role in shaping the system it seeks to describe: The research tool has become an unintended policy lever' (McCormick, 2000b: 5).

For these reasons the classification is under review (http://www.carnegiefoundation.org/whatsnew/index.htm). Minor changes were made to the classification in 2000, but more significantly a major review will result in 2005 in a 'Classification system that will replace the present single scheme with a series of classifications that will recognize the many dimensions of institutional commonality and difference' (Shulman, 2000: 2).

Build it into the (statutory) definitions of a degree
This is done in the New Zealand 1990 Act (Woodhouse, 1998). Indeed focusing on the characteristics of a degree may have greater force in that it

can ensure a focus at the level of the student experience and better ensure the effective interdependence of teaching, research and scholarship. In that context the New Zealand 1990 Act may not be such a positive model in that much of the focus is on staff being involved in research, and not so directly on what students experience of that research. The Act does include the statement that a degree is a qualification 'following a course of advanced learning' (Woodhouse, 1998), but seemingly leaves unstated what is meant by 'advanced learning'.

Recently in the UK, from our perspective a very positive development has been the Quality Assurance Agency's (2001) development work with the higher education community to create a framework for higher education qualifications and awards. Clearly this framework needs to be seen in the context of the move to a mass higher education system, including the strengthening of the links between further and higher education and the growth of postgraduate studies and work based learning. In that context there is a clear need to define what is meant by 'higher' education. The framework sets out a descriptor of academic levels, and these descriptors provide institutions with reference points or a map to use in internal and external audits, to review how students are being supported through the curriculum, and how students perform and are taught and assessed at those levels. The intent is to encourage the 'academic community into dialogue with itself and the translation of the traditionally implicit into more explicit form... [these] infrastructural activities create structures and activities that encourage, or induce academics into mapping and interrogating their own tacit practices and underlying assumptions' (Wright and Williams, 2001: 12).

In the context of our concerns here, the framework challenges and supports course teams and institutions to make more explicit and transparent what these course teams profess about the teaching–research nexus. Brief extracts from the framework in the case study below indicate how, by focusing on what the student experiences, it moves to significantly support the nexus as a characteristic of higher education. However, what it does not do – which clearly the New Zealand Act does – is spell out for institutions and for national policies with respect to funding the implications for university staffing policies. Possibly that will come later.

THE QUALITY ASSURANCE AGENCY'S (2001) FRAMEWORK FOR HIGHER EDUCATION QUALIFICATIONS IN ENGLAND, WALES AND NORTHERN IRELAND (HTTP://WWW.QAA.AC.UK/ CRNTWORK/NQF/EWNI2001/EWNI-TEXTONLY.HTM)

Selected extracts from QAA (2000: 7):

The higher education qualifications awarded by universities and colleges are at five levels. In ascending order, these are the Certificate, Intermediate, Honours, Masters and Doctoral levels.

The holder of a Certificate of Higher Education will have a sound knowledge of the basic concepts of a subject, and will have learned how to take different approaches to solving problems...

Holders of qualifications (at Intermediate level) will have developed a sound understanding of the principles in their field of study, and will have learned to apply those principles more widely. Through this, they will have learned to evaluate the appropriateness of different approaches to solving problems.

An Honours graduate will have developed an understanding of a complex body of knowledge, some of it at the current boundaries of an academic discipline. Through this, the graduate will have developed analytical techniques and problem-solving skills that can be applied in many types of employment. The graduate will be able to evaluate evidence, arguments and assumptions, to reach sound judgements, and to communicate effectively.

Much of the study undertaken at Masters level will have been at, or informed by, the forefront of an academic or professional discipline. Students will have shown originality in the application of knowledge, and they will understand how the boundaries of knowledge are advanced through research. They will be able to deal with complex issues both systematically and creatively, and they will show originality in tackling and solving problems.

Doctorates are awarded for the creation and interpretation of knowledge, which extends the forefront of a discipline, usually through original research. Holders of doctorates will be able to conceptualise, design and implement projects for the generation of significant new knowledge and/or understanding.

Linked to this programme level framework are statements known as subject benchmarks. These statements were formulated by groups of academics from the discipline. In some cases they were developed in conjunction with discipline based professional organizations. They describe the characteristics and standards of learning at the level of the honours degree in the various disciplines.

Subject benchmarking statements are intended to embody the:

- defining principles or essence of a subject;

- nature and extent of a subject, the map of subject territory, its boundaries and the range of programmes included in the territory;

- attributes that a graduate in the subject might be expected to display and demonstrate in terms of the subject knowledge and understanding subject skills and other skills and the teaching, learning and assessment methods which develop these attributes.

- the criteria that would be used to determine whether a graduate satisfied the 'threshold' standard for the award of an honours degree in the subject.

Many, perhaps all, of these statements emphasize aspects of the nexus as central to the requirements for honours classification in that discipline (http://www.qaa.ac.uk/crntwork/benchmark/benchmarking.htm). Thus the benchmarking statement for English states that honours graduates 'will be able to conduct research through self-formulated questions, supported by the gathering of relevant information and materials and organized lines of enquiry, resulting in a sustained piece or pieces of work of sustained argumentative and analytical power'.

Build in requirements for students being involved in research, using research or understanding research

Professional bodies can make these degree characteristics conditions for accrediting university degrees for professional recognition. These requirements will vary between using research, understanding research evidence and doing research reflecting professional values, but they can direct emphasis to the nexus. Such requirements often focus on the student experience or certainly the content of the curriculum. They can also focus on the experience that staff have in conducting research or scholarly activity. The British Psychological Society's (1995) procedures for reviewing undergraduate courses to ensure that graduates can then apply for graduate membership of the Society (and later qualify as a Chartered Psychologist) clearly support the nexus. Two central requirements are first, while courses and institutions have some freedom in determining the content of the curriculum, 'research design and analysis... must be covered.... An essential feature of the Qualifying Examination is the assessment of practical work that has to be completed covering research design and analysis' (pp 2–3). Second, 'eligibility for Graduate Membership.... The GQAC will thus be seeking to satisfy itself that the psychologists on the staff are sufficiently diverse in their areas of expertise to deliver a course that has sufficient depth at honours level' (p 3).

The UK Central Council for Nursing, Midwifery and Health Visiting's (2000) Requirements for accrediting, pre-registration and nursing programmes include:

> Safe and effective practice requires a sound underpinning of the theoretical knowledge, which informs practice, such knowledge must therefore be directly related to, and integrated with, practice in all programmes leading to registration as a nurse.

STRATEGY 2: ENSURE THERE ARE LIMITED NEGATIVE IMPACTS FROM RESEARCH SELECTIVITY

We have to recognize that all state systems will require research funds to universities to be selectively allocated to institutions, departments, disciplines and individuals. We recognize such selectivity as an effective political imperative in which we all have to operate. However we also think it incumbent on those shaping and determining national policies: that as a minimum they do so in ways which do not lead to a downplaying of individual, departmental and institutional priorities to teaching, and particularly in this context to a structural separation of student learning from (staff) research. Relatedly we think it unacceptable for national policy makers to take positions such as this one by the Higher Education Funding Council for England, which in its *Fundamental Review of Research* stated:

> Despite the evidence of a synergistic relationship between teaching and research, we make no recommendation about this: it would be wrong to allow teaching issues to influence the allocation of funds for research.
> (HEFCE, 2000b: 26)

Judgements and values such as this ignore the gains that students and society can get from research and see research as quite separate from other policies and policy initiatives. Politically, perhaps such a perspective questions why universities should do research, or reinforces a view that this would be better done in separate research organizations.

In our judgement the research and scholarly evidence is pretty conclusive that in Australia, the UK and the United States (and no doubt elsewhere) research selectivity is having negative impacts in causing individuals and institutions to neglect teaching and is threatening the teaching–research nexus for both students and staff.

Yet as this book was being written, in the UK the *Fundamental Review of Research* (HEFCE, 2000b: 2) concluded that 'HEFCE's present arrangements for research funding should stay broadly intact (and that) priority should be to protect grants for top-rated departments', a view that was confirmed after consultation with the sector (HEFCE, 2001). Such consultation was stated to be 'of interest to those responsible for research policy and funding'. Inside institutions, including Oxford Brookes, the views of the Research Committees were invariably sought, and teaching committees, mainstream academic staff, students, parents and taxpayers were *not* consulted. However, as we discussed in the review of the research evidence in chapter 2, research that the Funding Council had itself commissioned showed that the funding rewards the RAE offered led, at the level of the individual, the department and the institution, to 'a gradual separation, structurally of research from teaching' (McNay, 1998). Department heads reported that: 'good researchers spend less time teaching... and more undergraduate teaching is done by part-timers and postgraduates' (p 199). Two years on, another HEFCE commissioned study (JM Consulting, 2000) of teaching–research relations – in the context of the HEFCE Review of Research – concluded that pressures on academic staff are tending to 'compartmentalize activity and may threaten the beneficial synergies of research, teaching and other activities'. In Lewis Elton's (2000) analysis this is one of the 'unintended' short term and now long term consequences of the RAE. Indeed the Manager of the 2001 RAE has acknowledged 'the tensions and divisions between teaching and research' (Rogers, 1999: 285–86). This tension is also apparent in a study of the impact of Teaching Quality Assessment in Scotland, where the researcher used semi-structured interviews with senior staff (Drennan, 2001).

Such negative impacts of research selectivity are certainly not confined to the UK and the peculiar funding arrangements of the RAE. In Australia 'performance funding' has become prominent since the 1990s. In particular there are strategic and financial benefits to institutions from Federal government performance funding for research through the 'research quantum', which rewards institutions for bringing in research income, publications and postgraduate research enrolments. A recent report on Australian higher education argued that these funding mechanisms were leading to a 'disjunction between the two core academic activities (of teaching and research) through mechanisms that tend more and more to treat them as discrete. Both parts of the scholarly enterprise need to be supported together' (Reid, 2001: 13). A related research study of the impact of these managerial systems by Neumann and Guthrie argued that these forces were resulting in:

Professionals experience a drive to define their activity as teaching *or* research, as opposed to teaching *and* research. This policy drive leads to a narrowing of professional activities into discrete categories. A

further consequence of this drive on the part of Canberra, may be the definition of higher education institutions into three categories, as either 'teaching' or 'research' universities, with a third group predominantly 'teaching' but undertaking some 'research'.
(Neumann and Guthrie, 2001: iii)

In the USA, while different funding and review arrangements prevail, the patterns of institutional and individual performance are similar (Patrick and Stanley, 1998). To return once again to Boyer's *Scholarship Reconsidered*, Boyer (1990: X1) commented that 'following the Second World War the faculty award system narrowed just at the very time the mission of higher education was expanding'. Driving this devaluing of teaching and the structural separation within universities between teaching and research was the increasing selective and significant financial rewards to be gained through competitive research allocations, in the US case fuelled by ('cold war') Federal government spending.

Below we set out ways we think will help us out of the dilemma of national systems attempting to deliver research selectivity and teaching equity. But first we need publicly to acknowledge the issue, and as SEDA in its response to the UK Fundamental Review of Research argued, 'The policy relationship between teaching and research should be strengthened rather than, as may result from the conclusions in this consultation, decoupled' (Staff and Educational Development Association, 2000: 4). In the UK recent pronouncements by Howard Newby, the new Chief Executive of the Funding Council, do offer some hope. He has stated:

At the moment, the RAE is the only funding mechanism that relates performance to reward in any meaningful way. This cannot be desirable. We need incentives to produce excellence, and reward performance, in areas other than basic and strategic research so that the RAE will not be the exclusive focus of rewarding quality.
(Newby, 2001: 15)

This at least in part recognizes, along with Laurel and Hardy, the mess that we have got ourselves into, what we now need to develop are strategies that will in part support the nexus, or at least not threaten it.

STRATEGY 3: REQUIRE RESEARCH SELECTIVITY TO SUPPORT RESEARCH AREAS THAT DIRECTLY SUPPORT THE NEXUS

One way to strengthen the policy and practice relationship between teaching and research is to design research selectivity in ways that support strategies to achieve this including the following.

Support discipline based pedagogic research

While this book focuses on linking teaching and discipline based research, we also recognize and value that one way for research selectivity to support the nexus is to explicitly recognize through funding and so on, discipline based pedagogic research. Yet it is clear that at least in the UK context, research selectivity exercises do not generally support discipline based staff researching pedagogy. This external lack of recognition is then paralleled within universities (Yorke, 2000).

Require applications for research awards, and in particular through national research selectivity exercises such as the RAE, to identify how undergraduate and postgraduate students benefit from staff research

They might perhaps also identify how the department seeks to minimize any possible negative impacts from staff research. This might at least alert departments to consider the issue, particularly if it was seen that in the context of making judgements about a department's research culture and organization, the impact on students was one of the factors affecting grading.

Make undergraduate student involvement a condition of some research awards

In the United States the National Science Foundation (NSF) (http://www.nsf.gov/) makes undergraduate student involvement a condition for some competitive research grants.

Target some competitive grants to institutions to support (undergraduate) student researchers

Thus one NSF programme in announcing one such round of grant awards to institutions states: 'Active research experience is one of the most effective techniques for attracting talented undergraduates to and retaining them in careers in mathematics, science and engineering. Too few such experiences are now available. The Research Experience for Undergraduates program (REU) is designed to help meet this need' (NSF, 1998: 1).

Target some competitive grants to institutions to support the nexus

If research is to be limited, and if national systems assume that competitive grants are one way of encouraging system wide change, then one logical way to develop the nexus is to target some competitive grants to institutions to support it. The National Science Foundation in its Strategic Plan identified as one of its four strategic goals to 'integrate research and education' (NSF, 1995: 2). From this value developed, in 1997, Recognition Awards for the Integration of Research and Education (RAIRE), created to identify and recognize research intensive universities that had been innovative and effective in promoting research and education (NSF, 1997). In 1998 the awards were extended to 'lower ranked' degree granting institutions. In addition there are related programmes such as 'Research at Undergraduate Institutions' and 'Collaborative Research at Undergraduate Institutions' that support institutional and departmental structures and activities that involve (undergraduate) students doing research. Some of these awards are particularly targeted at 'minority' and/or under-represented groups (NSF, 1997).

Target some competitive grants to individuals to support the nexus

Many state systems now have awards for individual staff for teaching. One strategy to support the nexus would be to limit such awards to staff who can demonstrate high level integration between teaching and research or a significant contribution to system wide integration. In 2002 the National Science Foundation awarded six scholars with the prestigious award of 'Directors Awards for Distinguished Teacher Scholars' (and US $300,000 each!) for their work in linking teaching and research (http://www.nsf.gov/od/lpa/news/02/pr0239.htm).

Ensure that textbooks and educational software are valued

Part of Boyer's (1990) concern in *Scholarship Reconsidered* was that the US funding system for research and linked university policies for promotion was resulting in a downplaying of the importance of integrative scholarship, including the writing of student textbooks. Textbooks, and now increasingly software and Web sites, are potentially central to the diffusion of research and for its integration into student learning throughout the national (and of course the international) educational system. In the UK, the fact that the RAE does not value these (unless they can be shown and perceived to be 'original enquiry') has been often commented on by the RAE's critics (for example, Jenkins, 1995b).

    There are also important disciplinary issues here, for the role of textbooks and disciplinary cultures and forms of communication shape the boundaries between textbooks and original enquiry. Thus in the humanities there is a more permeable boundary between 'research' and 'scholarship'. As the Arts and Humanities Research Board (1999: 3) commented, 'the definition of "teaching materials" (still more so textbooks) and the exclusion of them... from the definition of research for the RAE have been notoriously problematic'. In Hong Kong the way this issue was dealt with was to widen the definition of research to recognize all four of Boyer's scholarships, including the scholarship of integration (French *et al*, 1999). Perhaps this widens the definition of research too far, but is one attempt to solve an issue that all national systems have to resolve: how to value (and that means funding and rewarding staff) the integrative scholarship that links primary research to the wider academic community, and particularly in the context of this book, to student learning. This is now of particular importance given the growth of various forms of distance learning, and in particular the impact of the Internet in supporting student learning. But at present we have national funding systems that largely reward discovery research and not its effective dissemination and integration in the wider academic community and student learning.

Selectively use grants to build requirements for data from research studies to be widely available to teachers, scholars and students

Many research studies produce data or materials that are ideally suited for other lecturers and students to analyse and use to carry out enquiry based learning. Many research active staff, in devising curricula, have students take their data and then analyse it in carrying out research based learning (see chapter 4). This could be supported by national or international research funders. In the UK (and no doubt elsewhere) it is a condition of Research Council funding that all data sets derived from a research project are to be lodged in a research archive, usually within the higher education community. This could be extended to making a portion of funding conditional on developing linked curricular materials and support, considering how the raw data and materials could be presented in such a way that undergraduates and postgraduates can do research using these sources.

Again this is where the Internet opens up major possibilities. Take the example of the Corvey Women Writers on the Web Project at Sheffield Hallam University (http://www.shu.ac.uk/corvey/). Based on a collection of Romantic era literature in a German library, and largely funded through the UK Arts and Humanities Research Board, the Corvey Project is developing a database of Romantic era women writers and selected texts. This research resource is specially designed to support students in researching and publishing using this material. An electronic journal *Corinne: Undergraduate Research on Romantic-Era Literature* (http://www.shu.ac.uk/corvey/corinne/) supports students and staff publishing their research. Staff at Sheffield Hallam have developed specialist dissertation (or capstone) modules using this material. This module, 'Explorations in Literary Culture 1790–1840', has students adopting a text or author and producing an individually negotiated portfolio of work that contains source documents in digitized form, a literary historical survey and a critical analysis (http://www.shu.ac.uk/schools/cs/english/year2/explit.htm). Condron (2000, http://cti-psy.york.ac.uk/aster/resources/case_studies/reports/ox_03/ox_03.html) provides an excellent analysis of this project. There are certain similarities between this project's concern to get students to understand the research process and the case studies (described in chapter 4) of geography courses that focus on (interviewing) individual academics. Though the Corvey project is based clearly in the humanities its ideas can be readily adapted to other disciplinary areas, by both academics and (national) funding agencies.

Harness the Internet to foster the nexus

The discussion of the Corvey project points to the immense potential the Web offers to enable research materials and support to be available nationally and internationally to both academics and students. Furthermore, given the central roles governments (including those sections of them concerned with higher education) play in both funding and organizing electronic resources, then there are clear policy levers that could ensure that such national and international funding organizations do support the nexus. Clearly here librarians and museum curators become centre stage in developing effective policies. There is scope for joint programmes between national systems. The next case study indicates the potential in such policies. That others will soon join such a case study in the UK (and no doubt elsewhere) is clearly suggested by a recent review of the Joint Information Systems Committee (Follet, 2000). This review called for JISC to add to its previous responsibilities for ensuring high level computing and information systems for supporting research, a concern for teaching materials in higher and further education (http://www.jisc.ac.uk/pub01/follett.html).

NATIONAL SCIENCE FOUNDATION AND JOINT INFORMATION SYSTEMS COMMITTEE: DIGITAL LIBRARIES AND THE CLASSROOM: TEST BEDS FOR TRANSFORMING TEACHING AND LEARNING

The United States National Science Foundation (NSF) and the United Kingdom Joint Information Systems Committee (JISC) successfully collaborated in funding a range of digital library projects in 1999 to 2001 (http://www.dli2.nsf.gov). They were focused on supporting research. In 2001 they announced a joint programme of activities in US and UK universities aimed at supporting teaching based on electronically available research materials (http://www.dli2.nsf.gov/internationalprojects/nsfjiscpre-announcement.html).

- Four exemplar projects of up to £1.5 million (US$2.1 million) each over three years will be funded to demonstrate how the education process for undergraduate students can be transformed using innovative applications of emerging information technologies and Internet resources.

- In creating the new courses, projects will be expected to examine many aspects of the whole learning process, including how the student experience can be enriched through the use of appropriate applications and access to electronic resources, the staff development needs of the teaching staff, the information service support teams and administrators, and consideration of the reward mechanisms for staff engaged in innovative activities.

- Four exemplar projects will be funded, where each project is a collaboration between at least one institution of higher education in the United States and one in the UK.

Some of the ideas in this section are clearly speculative. Some of the ideas, such as those developed by the National Science Foundation, are well developed, whereas some of the strategies such as the joint NSF/JISC electronic library and curricula projects are in their infancy. But surely, finding strategies that ensure that at minimum research selectivity does not harm teaching, and at best it selectively supports it, is a pressing priority for all national systems.

STRATEGY 4: FUND AND SUPPORT ALL INSTITUTIONS AND STAFF FOR (DISCIPLINE BASED) SCHOLARLY ACTIVITY

Whether all individual academic staff in all higher education institutions need currently to be doing original research is at best doubtful, both from the research evidence set out in chapter 2, and from the political realities of the national funding of mass higher education systems. However, we can start from the common sense assumption, and the research evidence, that academic staff need to be aware of current research and knowledge in their discipline, and more speculatively in the teaching of their discipline. Boyer's (1990) call in *Scholarship Reconsidered* for attention to the 'scholarship of teaching' has now been followed by much thinking as to the meaning of this term and how staff scholarship might be developed. This thinking and scholarly discussion has been a feature of the work in the United States (for example, Glassick, Huber and Maeroff, 1997; Huber, 2000; Huber and Morreale, 2002; Hutchings and Shulman, 1999), in Australia (Martin *et al*, 1999) and the UK, and internationally with respect to the disciplinary communities (Healey, 2000).

We saw in chapter 5 how three Australian universities without a national support structure had effectively used the Boyer and Carnegie ideas to develop their institutional policies in ways that gave substance to the scholarship of teaching (Zubrick, Reid and Rossiter, 2001). Our immediate concern here is to consider what national policies can do to support the scholarship of teaching in ways that enable effective linkages between teaching and research. Here it is significant to note that one of the tensions and issues in the scholarship of teaching is whether its focus is to encourage excellent classroom teaching, promotion structures and institutional policies that reward such 'excellent teaching', or the extent to which it requires teachers individually and collectively to make excellent teaching *public* through portfolios, writing student textbooks, learning software and publishing on (discipline based) pedagogy. The Carnegie Academy for the Scholarship of Teaching and Learning (CASTL) provides from the diverse and more privately funded US higher education system a model that other systems could adapt to their funding and cultures (see the case study in the box). CASTL is particularly important, for in cooperation with the American Association for Higher Education (AAHE); it has in part focused on how institutional and departmental policies can give substance to the ideas sketched out in *Scholarship Reconsidered* (Boyer, 1990). For example the AAHE's annual Faculty Roles and Rewards Conference in 2000 was specifically focused on reviewing the progress made particularly in institutional policies in realizing the scholarship of teaching (Jenkins, 2000).

THE CARNEGIE ACADEMY FOR THE SCHOLARSHIP OF TEACHING AND LEARNING (CASTL)

(http://www.carnegiefoundation.org/CASTL/highered/index.htm)

- Founded in 1998 and jointly funded by the Carnegie Foundation for the Advancement of Teaching and the Pew Charitable Trusts.

- Central goals are to: first, 'foster significant, long lasting learning for all students, second, enhance the practice and the profession of teaching and third, bring to faculty members work as teachers the recognition and awards afforded to other forms of scholarly work in higher education' (Carnegie Academy, 1999: 3).

- The goal is to 'render teaching public, subject to critical evaluation, and usable by others in both the scholarly and the general community' (p 3). This perspective is currently developed in the three components of this programme, and clearly such programmes may change.

- *The Pew National Fellowship Program for Carnegie Scholars* brings together 20 scholars annually to 'create and disseminate examples of

---

the scholarship of teaching and learning that contribute to thought and practice in the field' (p 4).

- *The Teaching Academy Campus Program* is 'designed for institutions of all types that are prepared to make a public commitment to foster and support the scholarship of teaching and learning on their campuses' (p 11). These programmes generally start with processes and structures to develop a shared language to discuss such issues, and other measures that are congruent with the suggestions on institutional strategies to enhance the teaching–research nexus suggested in chapter 5.

- *Work with the scholarly and professional societies.* This aspect of the programme focuses on working with organizations such as the American Sociological Association and others in ways that further embed the scholarship of teaching (see later discussion of this strategy).

Much of the work by the Carnegie Academy and others about the scholarship of teaching is aimed at improving teaching by making it 'scholarly'; it does not directly seek to address the teaching–research nexus. It does though connect with the teaching and research nexus in the following ways. Clearly it is open to institutions and departments worldwide with a particular mission of linking teaching and research to develop this, as did those three Australian institutions discussed in chapter 5 (Zubrick, Reid and Rossiter, 2000). But most of all, while the push for research selectivity directs attention and resources to the staff doing research, and can readily result in that research being disconnected with student learning and other academic staff, a concern for the scholarship of teaching and the scholarship of discipline based pedagogy (Healey and Jenkins, in press) can focus the attention of national systems (and institutions and others) on scholarship (and research?) for *all* staff. It thus offers the prospect of ensuring that students in all institutions gain from research based learning.

To return to the UK, the *Fundamental Review of Research* (HEFCE, 2000b: 4, para 23), did offer a way forward when it stated: 'Teaching needs scholarship.... What is required is for teaching to be animated by scholarship, and for scholarship in turn to be informed by research.' However, some of the difficulties in this view are brought out in the full paragraph from which the quote comes, and we think the issues here are relevant to all national systems.

Most academics argue that good research is necessary for good teaching. However there is a difference between academics being engaged in creating new knowledge themselves, and being alert to developments in their subject, including new discoveries, so that they can interpret and reinterpret the knowledge base of their subject to inform their teaching. Teaching needs scholarship, and scholarship depends on, and is distinct from, research. What is required is for teaching to be animated by scholarship, and for scholarship in turn to be informed by research. We propose that HEFCE should make it clear that its funds for teaching include an element to support scholarship. (HEFCE, 2000b: 4, para 23)

This supports the nexus by stating its importance and the role of staff scholarship and research in supporting teaching–research linkages. It certainly moves us to consider how national systems could ensure such research and scholarship. It seeks to direct these discussions into ensuring that institutions develop effective staff development policies and course review mechanisms to support these goals. However, we believe it draws a tighter distinction between teaching and research than is supported by the research evidence (see chapter 2 and in particular the research by Moses (1990)). Perhaps drawing this tight distinction between teaching and research is politically and financially useful to the policy makers, and the powerful elite research institutions and the top researchers outside the elite institutions. Indeed in confrontational mode we think such a statement is 'unscholarly' in that it asserts a position without really positioning it in the research literature, and at the same time ignores the evidence that questions or refutes that position. This is not evidence based policy making! The fear that this is a highly politicized reading of the research evidence is supported by the way forward proposed by HEFCE to recognize the role of scholarship in making it 'clear that its funds for teaching include an element to support scholarship' (HEFCE, 2000b). For that effectively says that research and teaching are conceptually and organizationally separate (see chapter 2), and more dangerously that such a separation justifies at national and institutional levels, that research policy, and in particular the research budget, is protected to support the few staff, with at best incidental benefit to students.

Recognizing as we do that there are distinctions between research, scholarship and student learning, nowhere in the policies then proposed are there ideas and policies to better connect them. While by stating in benign tones that the teaching budget is to support scholarship, the effect may well be inside institutions and departments to further drive a wedge between teaching and research. Institutional managers are likely to react by further restricting research funding to the few, putting higher teaching loads on the many and then bullying them through appraisal and so on to work even longer hours to produce evidence of 'scholarship'. Meanwhile those staff seeking to combine quality research and quality teaching will work and work. The system will have accentuated many of the problems of staff morale and working conditions we sketched in chapter 3.

We recognize that our immediate concerns here are shaped by working in the UK system and its immediate (2000–02) developments, and by working in an institution outside the research elite. However, we also assert that the issues the UK *Fundamental Review of Research* raises are of long term and worldwide importance to the nexus.

Possible ways forward that national systems worldwide could consider to ensure scholarship for all (while recognizing research selectivity) include:

- *Raise taxes and funding to support such scholarship for all staff,* and then of course ensure that all staff and students benefit from such funding and scholarship. Certainly in the UK the underfunding of higher education exacerbates many of these issues.

- *Restrict research funding to the elite institutions and departments,* but then ensure that they are responsible for effectively disseminating that research to other scholars and students in the national and international systems. (Such dissemination could include involving certain staff outside the research elite in this research and its public dissemination.)

- *Target special funds to support scholarship outside the research elite.* In effect this was what in the UK Dearing (NCIHE, 1997) proposed: following a visit to the United States he was 'persuaded... of the important role of research and scholarship in informing and enhancing teaching' (para 8.7) and proposed special funding to support such research/scholarship outside the research elite (see chapter 2).

- *Develop special funding streams to support all staff as scholars of their discipline, and the teaching of their discipline.* Perhaps such funding could enable all staff to have periodic sabbaticals to engage in high level public scholarship and research. This would recognize – as does the English Funding Council – that 'the opportunity to do research is an important reason why people decide on an academic career' (HEFCE, 2000b: 4). These opportunities should not be for the few, because the main losers will be students and society at large.

- *This funding could reward or even require staff to be professionally aware of the current research in their discipline* and be engaged in public discussion and dissemination of this research, including dissemination through teaching. This funding could require institutions to have structures and policies to support all staff as scholars, and as with some other professions require evidence of professional updating on both discipline-based pedagogy and discipline based research. This issue is developed below.

- *Require institutions to support such scholarship for all: and make that a condition of accreditation of their degrees and their national funding.*

- *Research the effectiveness of such policies.*

- *Build national schemes to accredit and support professional updating,* in cooperation with the national professional disciplinary organizations and
  the national development organizations. Build financial rewards into
  these schemes and ensure that they in part address how staff are
  supporting students' knowledge of, and involvement in, research.
  These requirements were significantly absent from the UK based
  Institute for Learning and Teaching's (ILT) original accreditation
  requirements or the SEDA system for the initial accreditation for new
  staff, but such a requirement could be readily built into these schemes,
  and their international counterparts. It could certainly be central to any
  advanced requirement concerning teaching. It would have system-wide
  impact if such a requirement were built into requirements for professional updating, as for example in the UK through the Institute for
  Learning and Teaching.

Indeed, just as this book was going to press the ILT (*ILT News*, 2002) introduced the following requirement for those seeking individual entry.

> *Section 6. Integration of scholarship, research and professional activities with*
> *teaching and support learning*
> (http://www.ilt.ac.uk/news/n20020708.html)
>   Please use this section to give examples of ways in which you draw
> on your subject research, scholarly activity or other professional activ-
> ities in the support of teaching and learning. Activities undertaken as
> part of a group or team are valued as much as individual activities.
> The ILT does not require all members to be significantly involved in
> discipline based research. If your main responsibilities lie outside this
> area, please indicate how you support your teaching and support of
> learning through other types of scholarly activity related to your disci-
> pline. Relevant professional activities may include those you engage
> in outside the higher education context.
>   The accreditors will expect to see evidence that you have actively
> sought opportunities to create links between your teaching and
> support for learners and your research and scholarly activity or
> relevant professional engagement with your discipline.

At present this is just for those staff seeking individual entry. It does not (as
yet?) impact on the accreditation of those courses for new staff that are
accredited by the ILT. But a suggestion of what may come is indicated by
the press release statement that 'the new process is designed to articulate
with the ILT's emerging CPD framework'. Thus, and this is conjecture, one

could envisage that this could be a central element of such a framework and be developed in the UK in conjunction with the new Subject Centres and disciplinary associations. It is also a framework that could be adapted by other national systems, and indeed by institutions and departments (http://www.ilt.ac.uk/news/n20020708.html).

In presenting these ideas we recognize them to be speculative, requiring detailed consideration and uncertain in effect: but the issue of ensuring scholarship and involvement with research for all staff is central to achieving the teaching–research nexus, as is rigorously researching the effectiveness of such policies. Certainly in the UK we have been preoccupied with high level research for few staff and with no effective consideration as to how (undergraduate) students should benefit from that research. In the UK we have also been preoccupied too with generic initial 'training' in teaching and have neglected the discipline based and scholarly (curricular) concerns of established staff (Healey and Jenkins, in press). Focusing internationally on how to ensure the 'scholarship of integration' for all, and ensuring that is effectively integrated with the 'scholarship of discovery', is central to realizing the teaching–research nexus, an effective higher education for all students, and a rewarding and an effective working environment for academic staff.

STRATEGY 5: DEVELOP EXTERNAL REVIEWS OF TEACHING AND RESEARCH THAT EXPLICITLY SUPPORT THE LINKAGE

In many state systems research and teaching are evaluated separately by national agencies. In Australia the Research Quantum assesses institutional performance on research (and allocates funds competitively on the basis of these returns); and teaching is nationally audited through the requirements on institutions to use the 'course experience questionnaire' to monitor student perceptions of the quality of their teaching. These results are publicly available, but there are no (direct) funding implications of such reviews of teaching. In the UK we have quite separate external reviews of research (through the RAE with its significant rewards for high scoring departments and no requirements for considering impacts on teaching) and a separate system for assessing the quality of teaching (with no explicit requirements to consider how this is linked to policies for research and scholarship). There are related criticisms of other national review systems. A recent review of the US quality assurance system criticized it for being bureaucratic, poorly linked 'into the life of the institution... [and] rarely seen to stimulate faculty to improve teaching and learning' (Dill, 2000: 35). Much of the discussion on how to rate US research universities is locked into issues that totally fail to consider whether their research reputations or 'outputs' have any benefits for students or for academics outside the research elite (Diamond and Graham, 2000, and see the previous discussion in this chapter on the negative effects of the Carnegie classification).

In terms of how such reviews and ratings affect whether the national system promotes effective teaching–research linkages, the following criticisms seem valid. First, in relation to the research evidence presented in chapter 2, they treat teaching and research as separate categories and have no effective conceptual frameworks or policy levers to promote the nexus, and second, often (as with the UK RAE and the Australian Research Quantum), they give limited but real financial rewards for research performance, and in effect encourage a decoupling of teaching from research inside institutions and departments.

There are three broad strategies for using external reviews to support the teaching–research nexus:

- Make limited adjustments to separate reviews of teaching and research.

- Focus the reviews, or periodic reviews, on the nexus.

- At institutional level, reviews should focus on the nexus as it is 'professed' by that institution.

Clearly whichever of these approaches are taken will have significant impacts on how institutions, departments and course teams operate, and what students experience.

Make limited adjustments to separate reviews of teaching and research

We have already in part discussed how external reviews of research could selectively support the nexus such as:

- with the Hong Kong RAE (French *et al*, 1999) clearly valuing high level integrative scholarly textbooks and e-learning resources;

- through explicitly requiring departments to state how their organization of research supports teaching (or does not harm it!);

- or using external assessments of teaching, which could seek student perceptions of the extent to which they experienced research based learning;

- or submissions of stated policy and practice that explicitly address the nexus and provide research based evidence of their effectiveness;

- or the support for scholarly activity by all staff (including part-time, visiting staff) being be a central concern.

All of these measures, and no doubt others, will take us further in realizing the nexus. Also they have the strength of improving the current systems rather than developing something untried. But the New Zealand system described below is not an untried methodology!

Focus the reviews, or periodic reviews, on the nexus

Occasionally nationally organized reviews may touch on the link, as have institutional Audits in the UK where a university has claimed a strong teaching–research nexus. Also in the UK the subject based Quality Assurance System for teaching considered the link in those departments and disciplines that claimed it existed. However to our knowledge, New Zealand is unusual and probably unique in having had a whole system review of how universities are addressing the teaching–research nexus. Clearly the New Zealand system is quite particular in a variety of ways, including the requirement through the 1990 Education Act that in universities 'research and teaching are closely interdependent' (cited in Woodhouse, 1998: 41) and the small size of the system, with eight universities, and the degree-granting polytechnics and colleges not having such a statutory requirement or being audited through this process. But the basic approach could be considered and adapted by other systems. Judging from the evidence, inside universities the impact has been to support the nexus. But to add a cautionary note there have been 'recent government signals to consider separate funding of teaching and research' (Willis, 2001: 2) an issue to which we will return. Perhaps these signals are an indication why national systems and individual universities and departments should vigorously develop the linkages to head off such moves by governments. It may be significant, particularly for Australian universities, that David Woodhouse, the Director who oversaw the teaching–research audit described below, took on a similar role for audit in Australia as foundation Director of the Australian Universities Quality Agency in 2001.

Auditing the teaching–research nexus in New Zealand

- The New Zealand Vice Chancellors Committee set up the Academic Audit Unit (AAU) to carry out quality audits of each university (Woodhouse, 1998; Meade and Woodhouse, 2000; Woodhouse, 2001).

- In 1998 it decided that the audit cycle for 2000–01 would be theme audits of every university on the linked issues of first, provision and support for postgraduate students, second, the research–teaching link (at undergraduate, as well as postgraduate level) and third, research policy, management and performance.

- The focus on the research–teaching link was partly prompted by the view that 'there is little international experience to draw on in auditing institutional quality processes in either research plus teaching or research *per se*. The work that has been done on the research–teaching link tends to focus on its existence, rather than its quality or utility' (Woodhouse, 1998: 42).

- Universities were to prepare for the review by auditing and reviewing their own work in achieving the nexus; and had to produce and publish a portfolio of evidence of what they had accomplished and were developing in support of the nexus.

- The audit manual that guided them suggested they considered the following indicators of the nexus:

  1. Specific linking of teaching and research in the institutional plan.

  2. Appointment, promotion and development of policies that encourage links.

  3. Active researchers who are involved in teaching at all levels.

  4. Encouragement of research into teaching and learning in a discipline.

  5. Performance Indicators used to check the effectiveness of institutional policies.

- The evidence from the portfolios themselves (some of which are available as are the subsequent institutional audits on the Web (http://www.aau.ac.nz/); also see the review of these audits by the University of Sydney (http://www.usyd.edu.au/about/quality/resources/ nzaau_resources.shtml)) is that the process prompted institutions to varying extents to consider measures to examine and indeed strengthen the nexus. See for example the case studies of Massey and Auckland set out in chapter 5. As Willis, an educational developer at the University of Wellington, states in a preliminary analysis of the impact of this audit, 'it is clear that one of the most useful outcomes of the process has been the diversity of activities undertaken in *preparation* for the audit' (Willis, 2001: 6; emphasis added).

- Willis further comments that most universities are now 'just beginning to understand the complexity of teaching /research links and need time and further encouragement to refine their approach' (p 8).

David Woodhouse's (2001: 12–13) (http://cedir.uow.edu.au/nexus/ dwoodhse.html) perspective on the impact of the review sees the central results, and explicitly their implications for other national systems, as follows:

- 'The selection of the teaching–research link as one audit focus triggered a great deal of thought about the underlying concept, about ways of interpreting it, and about its consequences.

- *Explicit attention is being paid to what academics mean when they claim a link between teaching and research, with attempts to explicate it and its supposed benefits. This is the most important and potentially useful finding* (our emphasis).

- The concept of research for the purpose of its relation to teaching is being broadened from referring to *product* only, to include research and teaching *process* and *culture*.

- The observed increase in teaching only and research only staff means that the rationale, intent and consequences of the link must be considered explicitly. It removes the ability to hide behind the false assumption that all academics are both teachers and researchers, and further that they all integrate their teaching and research in some way to the positive benefits of one or both these activities.

- Incentives are being introduced for linking teaching and research, and making the link explicit.'

At institutional level, reviews should focus on the nexus as it is 'professed' by that institution

A central theme of chapter 5 was that institutions should develop their own conceptions of the nexus, a perspective that is given extra salience as higher education national systems move towards supporting institutional diversity. Furthermore there are many who would agree with the interpretation offered here, that the traditional conception of the nexus at the level of the individual teacher is no longer sustainable in most institutions, that is, where individual academics are centrally involved in undergraduate teaching and research, and implicitly integrate these roles, if only through the highly selected students they taught. Now national systems need to recognize and support institutional diversity; but at the same time ensure that the nexus is supported in ways that are congruent with institutional missions and resources. That this is both possible and desirable is for example demonstrated in the Australian study of three contrasting institutions reported in chapter 5. Thus in elite research-rich institutions like the University of Western Australia, Cambridge and so on, they should be able to demonstrate a relatively traditional conception of the nexus, while elsewhere the focus might be at the level of the overall student experience, the immediate support of teacher–scholars or access to worldwide research through quality learning resources.

But this might mean that national audit and accreditation needs to be both more flexible in allowing institutional interpretations of the nexus and more rigorous in ensuring that this is not just mission rhetoric. This appears to be in part the approach being taken by the newly-established Australian Universities Quality Agency (http://www.auqa.edu.au/index. shtml), under the direction of David Woodhouse. That does not specify a particular requirement about the nexus but does clearly state that if an institution defines its view of quality in those terms then it has to demonstrate that its procedures support that view of quality. There are early indications that this approach is having some 'positive' impacts. Thus a recent Google search picked out the minutes from the Senate at one Australian research university stating:

> Reference was made to a draft audit manual recently released by the Australian Universities Quality Agency. When audited the University will need to prove its teaching research nexus.

STRATEGY 6: NATIONAL AND INTERNATIONAL DISCIPLINARY ORGANIZATIONS CAN SUPPORT THE NEXUS

In chapter 2 we showed how the research evidence points to the form of the teaching–research relationship being in part shaped by disciplinary concerns, for example, for evidence based practice in health care. For many academics their linkages are at national and international levels, through informal and formal ties and membership of professional organizations. With or without state support disciplinary organizations can do much to support the nexus, for example, through special conferences or sessions at national and international meetings; through special projects or interest groups; through theme issues of disciplinary pedagogic journals and /or special publications and Web sites, and so on. To take one disciplinary example, the European Society for Engineering Education (SEFI) (http://www.ntb.ch/SEFI/Index.html) developed in 1999 a new working group on 'Synergies between research and engineering education', and this then led to a range of articles in the society's professional journal, the *European Journal of Engineering Education* (for example, Seitzer, 2000; Oehme and Seitzer, 2000).

Certainly in the UK there is an opportunity here for the newly-established national Subject Centres (http://www.ltsn.ac.uk/), supported by national funding, to develop special initiatives to support the nexus in conjunction with their disciplinary networks. Given that disciplines, and some disciplinary associations, are international in focus, there is scope here for developing international networks and projects to support the nexus, though such international networks face the problem that most state funding is often restricted to the national level and many disciplinary organizations are immediately at national level. But such national professional associations will have personal and organizational links with those in other national systems, so these can work internationally to secure the links.

These disciplinary initiatives should of course include those generic or higher education organizations that bring together those (specialist) staff – educational developers and others – such as SEDA, POD, AAHE, HERDSA, STLHE and so on. They can play critical roles in bringing the generic research into the lives of academics; and networking expertise across the disciplines and different types of institutions, and developing projects and publications in support of the nexus. This publication is an example of how the UK based SEDA, a professional organization of educational and staff developers, has here supported the nexus.

STRATEGY 7: DEVELOP NATIONAL AND INTERNATIONAL ORGANIZATIONS AND PROJECTS TO SUPPORT THE NEXUS

Finally in considering this broad typology of national and international strategies, the nexus can be directly supported by specific projects, structures and organizations that operate at national and/or international levels, and this can be developed through centralized states such as the UK and the more private and diversely funded US system.

We have already drawn significantly on a range of national projects that have explicitly considered, and in cases sought to strengthen, the nexus. Boyer's (1990) *Scholarship Reconsidered* was explicitly supported, funded and disseminated by the Carnegie Foundation; and as we have seen further development and dissemination has been achieved through national organizations such as Carnegie itself, foundations such as Pew, and the American Association for Higher Education. In Australia on a more modest level the (Federal) Department of Education, Training and Youth Affairs (DETYA) funded the study by Zubrick, Reid and Rossiter (2001) on the nexus in three contrasting institutions. This book has also drawn on the study for the Funding Council by JM Consulting (2000) on how in the UK teaching–research relations were being shaped by institutional and national policies. These nationally funded studies and publications are important in both alerting institutional and national policy makers to (aspects of) the nexus: and in providing the policy climate for national actions and structures to strengthen the nexus. In demonstrating what national organizations can achieve we look at examples from two different systems, first the more centralized government based UK system and second, the more privately funded and diverse US system. These case studies demonstrate that national organizations can play a key role in realizing or rather supporting the nexus in institutions, disciplines, departments and individual courses.

Specific US national initiatives

Case study: Council for Undergraduate Research (CUR), Washington, DC (http://www.cur.org./)

- Significant national not-for-profit organization, mainly science based and in institutions outside the research elite.

- Washington, DC based since 1998, reflecting a central focus on communicating with Federal Agencies to raise awareness and funds.

- Mission as modified June 2001: 'to support and promote high-quality undergraduate student–faculty collaborative research and scholarship'.

- Origins (1978) and culture clearly in the sciences and of student as 'apprentice' to faculty; much of original stimulus was and is to raise awareness and obtain funds for research for undergraduate institutions outside the research elite.

- 'Has (as of 2001) moved into the social sciences: its mission statement reflects this and the possibility that it will soon encompass programs for the humanities. CUR has also opened the door wider to research universities; the new mission statement omits specific reference to predominantly undergraduate institutions though many of our programs still focus on these institutions' (Hoagland, 2001).

- Main financial support from institutional and individual members, plus corporate donors, (Federal) grants and private foundations.

- Flagship programme is the Undergraduate Summer Fellowships: 10 weeks' research with an academic mentor plus travel to present at a conference.

- National conferences for faculty and administrators.

- CUR works with institutions and faculty on writing grant proposals, and improving institutional and department undergraduate research programmes.

- A bi-annual meeting in Washington co-sponsored by a US Federal Agency focuses on informal networking with Federal officials, discussions on current science policy.

- Annual CUR Undergraduate Research Posters on the Hill: competitive awards for students who present and meet with State members of Congress to thank them for Federal funding and ask for further support!

- Various publications, including the *Council for Undergraduate Research Quarterly* (http://www.cur.org/Publications/Quarterlies.html) and *How to Develop and Administer Institutional Undergraduate Research Programs* (Hakim, 2000).

National Conference on Undergraduate Research (NCUR) (http://www.ncur.org//basics/index.htm)

- Has similar aims to CUR, supporting undergraduate research.

- NCUR aims to 'enrich undergraduate teaching and learning by providing opportunities to experience first hand the processes of scholarly exploration and discovery... encourage awareness of undergraduate research'.

- Does this principally through an annual national conference where students and staff mentors present their research, and often are financially supported to attend, networking meetings, special projects, publications and so on.

Reinvention Center at Stony Brook, and institutional 'consortia' (http://www.sunysb.edu/Reinventioncenter/)

- Based at the University of Stony Brook (New York), whose president S Strum Kenny chaired the Boyer Commission (University of Stony Brook, 1998) report on *Reinventing Undergraduate Education: A blueprint for America's research universities* (http://naples.cc.sunysb.edu/Pres/boyer.nsf/).

- The Reinvention Center was founded in 2000 to support the nexus in research intensive universities, but recognizing the ideas have implications for other institutions.

- Has promoted a range of informal regional discussions for institutional leaders in research universities.

- Has developed a Web site (including a database of innovations in undergraduate research based education), a listserve and symposia on aspects of undergraduate research and institutional policies etc.

- Has completed a study of the impact of the Boyer Commission (University of Stony Brook, 1998) on US research universities. Many now have developed programmes enabling undergraduates to do research and have made other related curricula changes (Wilson, 2002).

Case study: Project Kaleidoscope (http://www.pkal.org/)

- Aims at undergraduate courses in mathematics, engineering and science fields.

- Informal alliance of institutions, administrators and faculty.

- Current sponsors include National Science Foundation, US Department of Education, Exxon Mobil Foundation, Camille and Henry Dreyfus Foundation.

- The name 'Kaleidoscope' reflects the view that attention needs to be given to all facets of the undergraduate and institutional environments with a strong focus on institution-wide changes.

- Holds national and regional meetings, Web site and listserves, publications and so on.

Case study: Link (http://www.linkresearch.org/)

- Based in San Francisco with New York and Seattle 'outreach' offices, in the initial year was supported by Stanford University's School of Law.

- Supported by a range of foundations.

- Web based organization that links student (and faculty) researchers with non-profit organizations and public agencies.

- Students and staff want to do research; non-profit organizations need research to guide practice; Link facilitates connections between these two groups.

Specific UK national initiatives

Case study: maximizing the benefits to teaching of research (http://www2.open.ac.uk/cehep/educational/l_and_t_strats/index.htm)

- Aim to support those institutions whose institutional learning and teaching strategies specifically aim to link teaching and research.

- Project commissioned by the Higher Education Funded Council for England (HEFCE) and carried out by the National Co-ordination Team at the Open University directed by Graham Gibbs (2001–02).

- Gathering of case studies of interesting practice.

- Publication of an analysis of issues arising from this practice and case studies illustrating the principles in action.

- Regional events to engage those from institutions responsible for that strand of their learning and teaching strategy.

Project Link: linking teaching and research and consultancy in planning, land and property management, and building (http://www.brookes.ac.uk/schools/planning/LTRC/)

- A three-year (2000–03) project through HEFCE's Fund for the Development of Teaching and Learning. (This provides competitive funding for discipline based curriculum development projects: http://www.ncteam.ac.uk/projects/fdtl/index.htm.)

- A consortium of four institutions: Oxford Brookes, Sheffield Hallam, University of Westminster and the University of West of England.

- Aims include to 'identify, develop and disseminate good practice in linking teaching, research and consultancy' in the three closely related disciplines.

- Main focus is achieving this in these disciplines in the four institutions.

- Secondary foci on strengthening the nexus in these disciplines in about 10 cascade institutions, and across the institutions (potentially to all disciplines) in the four consortia institutions.

- Developing international disciplinary links through an International Advisory Panel and proposed discipline based international conference.

- Other 'outputs' include various publications and a Web site, which has a developing resources portfolio of effective practice.

Case study: linking teaching and research in the disciplines (http://www.brookes.ac.uk/genericlink/)

- National project (2002–03) for the Generic Subject Centre and Learning and Teaching Network (http://www.ltsn.ac.uk/genericcentre/default.asp).

- Creation of generic support materials (including Web site) to help further embed teaching–research links in disciplinary communities.

- Five Subject Centres embedding teaching–research links in their disciplinary communities (other Subject Centres to follow).

- Providing a framework, ideas and strategies that will also support other Subject Centres in developing such links.

IN CONCLUSION: RE-SHAPING THE LINK

In the introductory chapter we set out the aim of this book as 'to help individual staff, course teams, departments and national systems to make effective linkages between discipline based research and student learning'. We prefaced our discussion with what for us is a seminal perspective, Paul Ramsden's (2001: 4) view that, 'I believe that the main hope for realizing a genuinely student centred undergraduate education lies in re-engineering the teaching–research nexus.'

In concluding we restate our central themes and then indicate where we think developments now need to further build on this work, which has depended so much on the work of many academics worldwide. Central themes running through this book are these linked perspectives:

- the value judgements of the critical and central role of universities in helping students and society at large to both value and understand knowledge forged through research;

- that for many academic staff their own motivation as a teacher is linked to their involvement in discipline based research and scholarship;

- the strong research evidence that the teaching–research linkage is not automatic and indeed in many ways is problematic;

- the growing research evidence that staff research can aid student learning and motivate students;

- the recognition that the 'classical' form of the nexus with individual staff who are centrally involved in both teaching and research is not applicable in a mass higher education, except in selected institutions;

- that aspects of contemporary society, in particular issues of social, scientific and ethical complexity and the needs of a knowledge economy make the nexus, albeit transformed, vital to student learning;

- then what is perhaps the central theme, realizing that this valued potential teaching–research nexus requires action, in a whole variety of ways and levels, in ways that are congruent with the research evidence.

We have shown how individual staff, course teams, departments, national systems (and to an extent international organizations such as disciplinary communities), can do much to realize the linkages between staff research and student learning. Internationally we have much good practice in a whole series of contexts to build and act upon. *In part our energies should now largely focus on 'doing it' in our own particular context of course team, department, institution and role.* Here it is apposite to quote David Woodhouse's (2001: 13) conclusion on the impact and results of the New Zealand audit. 'These initiatives give cause for optimism about the future development and implementation of the teaching–research link.' We share that optimism, though tempered with a concern that national and institutional policy makers may not be willing to act to secure the nexus. As we have already acknowledged, working in the UK shapes our perceptions. If this chapter has an 'ogre' it is the UK Research Assessment Exercise, and if it has a 'heroine' or a sense of what should or could be, it is the New Zealand audit of teaching–research links.

To temper that optimism, we point out that in the final stages of writing this book, following a review of the whole system (Tertiary Education Advisory Commission, 2001) a draft Strategy for the New Zealand higher education system for the years 2002–07 was published (Office of the Associate Minister for Education, 2001). Pointing to the impacts of globalization and the needs of the 'knowledge economy', the draft strategy includes the strategic objectives of 'to put incentives in place within the tertiary funding model to reward excellent research; promote a more focused tertiary research investment through world class clusters of specialization and networks' (p 25) while also stating that 'research activity is also important for teaching at degree level and above, because new knowledge is incorporated into the scholarship activities of teachers.... This provides students with richer learning experiences, thereby increasing their capability' (p 55). Yet the final report of the Commission whose deliberations shaped this draft strategy states:

> The Commission recommends that the legislation requiring that degrees be taught mainly by people engaged in research be amended, to require undergraduate degrees to be taught by people who have a comprehensive and current knowledge of their discipline and the skills to communicate that knowledge.
>
> The imposition of tighter requirements that providers must fulfil before they can access funding for postgraduate teaching and supervision would ensure that such education occurs within an appropriate, high quality environment. The proposed Performance-Based Research Fund and both models of Centres and /Networks of Research Excellence would provide further important incentives for improving and maintaining the quality of research in the tertiary education system.
> (Tertiary Education Advisory Commission, 2001: X111, and see pp 107–14 for the overall discussion of this issue)

These developments (for in effect the focus of the nexus seems to have moved to postgraduate level and there its key role is to support research quality) reinforce a central concern of this and previous chapters: that holding on to the nexus in the context of a strategic concern to produce research excellence is a central dilemma for all state systems, and provides part of an agenda for others to follow up the concerns of this book. It also cautions our optimism for the future of the nexus.

There are however current developments to make us optimistic about a reshaped nexus. In particular this book has hopefully demonstrated the wisdom and ingenuity of academics worldwide in reshaping and developing the nexus. For example, in the United States there has been a strong growth in undergraduate research and the development of innovative year one and capstone courses that develop the call for more research based learning in the Boyer Commission (University of Stony Brook, 1998; Wilson, 2002). In Australia, the study of three very contrasting institutions (Zubrick, Reid and Rossiter, 2001) has shown how the nexus can be developed in very different institutional contexts. In New Zealand, institutions are progressing the link, building on what they have learnt from the system-wide audit. In Canada, institutions such as the University of British Columbia and McMaster are showing how 'inquiry' or research based learning can pervade the undergraduate curriculum. Meanwhile in the UK, there are growing calls to abolish or significantly reshape the RAE, partly because of its negative impacts on institutional concerns for teaching quality, including the negative impacts on teaching–research relations. The Funding Council is conducting, in 2002, a further strategic policy review 'with the aim of identifying priorities for the next five years', and in that context Sir Howard Newby, the Chief Executive, has stated that 'whether there will be an RAE in its present form is doubtful' (Newby, 2002: 13). Whether what emerges will support the nexus is clearly uncertain, but at least there is some space in the system to make these arguments.

In making these arguments worldwide we have to recognize that there are still gaps in our understanding and there are still significant areas to be developed. As this book has been based on the work of so many people, we conclude by suggesting some of the key areas that we think require further development.

As researchers, we feel there is still much to be explored. These include: the nature of teaching–research relationships in the disciplines; the impact of research based learning on student intellectual development; staff experience of teaching–research relations; and moving into the so far uncharted areas of department and institutional policies and cultures and their impact on the nexus, and how these policies and cultures can be re-shaped to support the nexus.

As academic staff, educational developers and policy makers we likewise have much to develop. Disciplinary communities need to share and develop good practice in embedding the link in their subjects and exploring what the link means in the different disciplines. Departments and institutions need similarly to develop and spread good practice, and institutional managers and national policy makers need to shape and monitor policies that explicitly support the link.

We are also aware that there are gaps or areas not sufficiently developed in this book. Inside universities the main focus has been on academic and managerial staff supporting the nexus, and the roles of librarians, information technology staff, technicians, student services and students themselves have perhaps been underplayed.

Nationally and internationally the immensely important role of publishing companies has been largely ignored, while the potential of international consortia of institutions and national systems has only been touched on. But that does bring us back to the importance of considering a large range of factors in realizing the nexus and assisting students and society at large to cope with and enjoy a world of supercomplexity.

However, as our readers you will have your views as to what should be done, and what we have failed to develop adequately here. We look forward to hearing about what you have added to this enterprise.

References

Al-Jumailly, A and Stonyer, H (2000) Beyond teaching and research: changing engineering academic work, *Global Journal of Engineering Education*, **4** (1), pp 89–97

Appleton, J V (2000) Research Education in the SHC: the story so far, Oxford Brookes University Third School of Health Care Research Conference, Oxford Brookes University, Oxford

Appleton, J V and Sanders, C (2000) *Research Education Steering Group Recommendations for the Future Delivery of Research Education in the School of Health Care*, Oxford Brookes University, Oxford

Astin, A W (1993) *What Matters In College? Four critical years revisited*, Jossey-Bass, San Francisco, Calif.

Astin, A W and Chang, M J (1995) Colleges that emphasize research and teaching: can you have your cake and eat it too? *Change*, **27** (5), pp 45–49

Austin, A E (1996) Institutional and departmental cultures: the relationship between teaching and research, *New Directions for Institutional Research*, **90**, pp 57–66

Bakker, G (1995) Using 'pedagogical-impact statements' to make teaching and research symbiotic activities, *Chronicle of Higher Education*, March

Bandura, A (1977) Self-efficacy: toward a unifying theory of behavioural change, *Psychological Review*, **84**, pp 191–215

Barff, R (1995) Small classes and research experiences for new undergraduates, *Journal of Geography in Higher Education*, **19** (3), pp 299–306

Barnett, R (1992) Linking teaching and research: a critical inquiry, *Journal of Higher Education*, **63** (6), pp 619–36

Barnett, R (2000) *Realizing the University in an Age of Supercomplexity*, Society for Research into Higher Education and Open University Press, Buckingham

Baxter Magolda, M B (1992) *Knowing and Reasoning in College: Gender-related patterns in students' intellectual development*, International Publishing Group, New York

Baxter Magolda, M B (1999a) *Creating Contexts for Learning and Self-Authorship*, Vanderbilt University Press, Nashville, Tenn.

Baxter Magolda, M B (1999b) *Impact of the Undergraduate Summer Scholar Experience on Epistemological Development*, University of Miami, Fla.

Baxter Magolda, M B (2001a) Interview with Alan Jenkins, April

Baxter Magolda, M B (2001b) *Making Their Own Way: Narratives for transforming higher education to promote self-development*, Stylus, Sterling, Va.

Beckhradnia, B (1998) The polarisation of teaching and research: false dichotomy, principled policy or damaging expedient? *Research and Scholarship*, Southampton Institute

Ben-David, J (1977) *Centres of Learning: Britain, France, Germany, United States*, McGraw-Hill, New York

Bender, C (1999) The development of an undergraduate research program in biology: a guide for the uninitiated, *Council on Undergraduate Research Quarterly*, **16** (2): 73–76

Bender, C, Ward, S and Wells, M A (1994) Improving undergraduate biology education in a large research university, *Molecular Biology of the Cell*, **5**, pp 129–34

Blackmore, P, Gibbs, G and Shrives, L (1999) *Supporting Staff Development within Departments*, Oxford Centre for Staff and Learning Development, Oxford

Boyer, E L (1987) *College: The undergraduate experience in America*, HarperCollins, New York

Boyer, E L (1990) *Scholarship Reconsidered: Priorities of the professoriate*, Carnegie Foundation for the Advancement of Teaching, Princeton, NJ

Breen, R and Lindsay, R (1999) Academic research and student motivation, *Studies In Higher Education*, **24** (1), pp 75–93

Brew, A (1999) The value of scholarship, paper presented at the Annual Conference of the Higher Education Research and Development Society of Australasia, Melbourne

Brew, A (2001a) *The Nature of Research: Inquiry in academic contexts*, Routledge Falmer, London

Brew, A (2001b) Developing new partnerships between teaching and research, Annual Conference of the Research and Development Society of Australasia, University of Newcastle, Newcastle, NSW

Brew, A and Boud, D (1995a) Teaching and research: establishing the vital link with learning, *Higher Education*, **29**, pp 261–73

Brew, A and Boud, D (1995b) Research and learning in higher education, in *Research Teaching and Learning in Higher Education*, ed B Smith and S Brown, pp 30–39, Kogan Page, London

British Psychological Society (1995) Accreditation of first qualifications in psychology [Online] www.bps.ac.uk

Brown, R (1999) Diversity in higher education: has it been and gone? *Higher Education Review*, **31** (3), pp 3–16

Brown, R B and McCartney, S (1998) The link between research and teaching: its purpose and implications, *Training and Technology International*, **35** (2), pp 117–29

Byrne, B J (1997) Infusing quantitative reasoning across the disciplines, in *Student Active Science: Models of innovation in college science teaching*, ed A P McNeal and C D'Avanzo, Saunders College Publishing, Fort Worth, Texas

Carnegie Academy (1999) *The Carnegie Academy for the Scholarship of Teaching and Learning*, American Association for Higher Education, Menlo Park, Calif.

Clark, B R (1987) The modern integration of research activities with learning and teaching, *Journal of Higher Education*, **68** (3), pp 242–55

Clark, B R (1993a) *The Research Foundations of Graduate Education: Germany, Britain, France, United States, Japan*, University of California Press, California

Clark, B R (1993b) The research foundations of post-graduate education, *Higher Education Quarterly*, **47** (4), pp 301–14

Clark, B R (1997) The modern integration of research activities with teaching and learning, *Journal of Higher Education*, **68** (3), pp 242–55

Coaldrake, P and Stedman, L (1999) *Academic Work in the Twenty-first Century: Changing roles and policies*, Higher Education Division, Department of Education, London

Coate, K, Barnett, R and Williams, G (2001) Relationships between teaching and research in higher education in England, *Higher Education Quarterly*, **55** (2), pp 158–74

Colbeck, C C (1998) Merging in a seamless blend, *Journal of Higher Education*, **69** (6), pp 647–71

Commonwealth of Australia (1999) *New Knowledge, New Opportunities*, Canberra

Condron, C (2000) *Integrating Research and Teaching: Using the Corvey Project to teach students research skills*, Project Aster, University of York [On line] http://cti-psy.york.ac.uk/asterresources/case studies/reports/ox 03/ox 03.html

Cooke, R (1998) Enhancing teaching quality, *Journal of Geography in Higher Education*, **22** (3), pp 283–84

Cosgrove, D (1981) Teaching geographical thought through student interviews, *Journal of Geography in Higher Education*, **5** (1), pp 19–22

Court, S (1996) The use of time by academic and related staff, *Higher Education Quarterly*, **50** (4), pp 237–60

Currie, J (2000) Exploit your experience, *Times Higher Education Supplement*, March p 40

Diamond, N and Graham, H D (2000) How should we rate research universities? *Change*, July/August, pp 20–33

Dill, D (2000) Is there an academic audit in your future? *Change*, **32** (4), pp 35–41

Downey, R G, Coffman, J R and Dyer, R A (2000) *Individualization of Faculty Work at Kansas State University*, American Association for Higher Education, New Orleans, La.

Drennan, L T (2001) Quality assessment and the tension between teaching and research, *Quality in Higher Education*, **7** (4), pp 167–78

Drennan, L T and Beck, M (2000) Teaching quality performance indicators: key influences on the UK universities' scores, *Quality Assurance in Education*, **9** (2), pp 92–102

Dwyer, C (2001) Linking research and teaching: a staff–student interview project, *Journal of Geography in Higher Education*, **25**, pp 357–76

Elowson, M and Gregerman, S (2001) Undergraduate research programs, conference presentation, Schreyer National Conference, Innovations in Undergraduate Research and Honors Education, Pennsylvania State University, March

Elton, L (1992) Research, teaching and scholarship in an expanding higher education system, *Higher Education*, **46** (3), pp 252–68

Elton, L (2000) *Funding Research and Teaching: Avoiding unintended consequences*, Learner-Centred Universities for the New Millennium, Frankfurt

Elton, L (2001) Research and teaching: conditions for a positive link, *Teaching in Higher Education*, **6**, pp 43–56

Entwistle, N (1995) The use of research on student learning in quality assessment, in *Improving Student Learning through Assessment and Evaluation*, ed G Gibbs Oxford Centre for Staff and Learning Development, Oxford

Entwhistle, N and Ramsden, P (1983) *Understanding Student Learning*, Croom Helm, London

Evans, C (1988) *Language People: The experience of teaching and learning modern languages in British universities,* Society for Research into Higher Education and Open University Press, Milton Keynes

Fairweather, J S (1993) Faculty rewards reconsidered: the nature of tradeoffs, *Change,* **25** (4), pp 44–47

Follett, B (2000) A Review of the Joint Information Systems Committee [Online] ww.jisc.ac.uk/pub01/follett.html

Forman, S G (2000) Developing research skills in undergraduates, Conference presentation at American Association for Higher Education, Faculty Roles and Rewards, New Orleans, February

French, N J, Ko, P K, Massey, W F, Siu, H F, and Young, K (1999) Research assessment in Hong Kong, *Journal of International Education,* pp 47–53

Garrick, J and Rhodes, C (eds) (2000) *Research and Knowledge at Work: Perspectives, case studies and innovative strategies,* Routledge, London

Gibbons, M *et al* (1994) *The New Production of Knowledge,* Sage, London

Gibbs, G (1995a) The relationship between quality in research and quality in teaching, *Quality in Higher Education,* **1** (2), pp 147–57

Gibbs, G (1995b) How can promoting excellent teachers promote excellent teaching? *Innovations in Education and Training International,* **32** (1), pp 74–82

Gibbs, G (2000) Are the pedagogies of the disciplines really different? in *Improving Student Learning Through the Disciplines,* ed C Rust, pp 41–51, Oxford Centre for Staff and Learning Development, Oxford

Gibbs, G (2001) *Analysis of Strategies for Learning and Teaching,* Higher Education Funding Council for England, Bristol

Glassick, C E, Huber, and Maeroff, G I (1997) *Scholarship Assessed: Evaluation of the professoriate,* Special Report of the Carnegie Foundation for the Advancement of Teaching, Jossey-Bass, San Francisco, Calif.

Griffiths, R (2002) Planning education for a knowledge-based society: strengthening the links between teaching and research, paper presented at the Planning Research Conference, Dundee, April

Haigh, N (2000) Everyday academic life as an expression of scholarship: a staff development perspective in Ernst Boyer's views, paper presented at ICED Annual Conference

Hakim, T M (2000) *How to Develop and Administer Institutional Undergraduate Research Programs,* Council for Undergraduate Research, Washington

Harley, H (2002) The impact of research selectivity on academic work and identity in UK universities, *Studies in Higher Education,* **27** (2), pp 187–205

Hattie, J and Marsh, H W (1996) The relationship between research and teaching: a meta-analysis, *Review of Educational Research,* **66** (4), pp 507–42

Healey, M (2000) Developing the scholarship of teaching: a discipline based approach, *Higher Education Research and Development,* **19** (2), pp 169–89

Healey, M and Jenkins, A (in press) Discipline-based educational development, in *The Scholarship of Academic Development,* ed R Macdonald and H Eggins, Open University Press, Milton Keynes

Hegarty, J R (1998) Teaching research methods by simulating the real-world research process, in *Innovations in Psychology Teaching,* Vol 104, ed J Radford, D V Laar and D Rose, Staff and Educational Development Association, Oxford

Henry, J (1995) *Teaching Through Projects*, Kogan Page, London

Hewton, E (1977) The curricular implications of concentrated study, *Studies in Higher Education*, **2** (1), pp 79–87

Higher Education Funding Council for England (HEFCE) (1995) *Report on Quality Assessment 1992–1995*, Higher Education Funding Council for England, Bristol

HEFCE (1999) *The Role of Selectivity and the Characteristics of Excellence with Regard to the Creation of Research Outputs and Research Training*, Higher Education Funding Council for England, Bristol

HEFCE (2000a) *Council Briefing* (29), pp 1–2, Higher Education Funding Council for England, Bristol

HEFCE (2000b) Review of research [Online] www.ilt.ac.uk/archives/hefce_rev.htm, Higher Education Funding Council for England, Bristol

HEFCE (2001) Strong support for continuation of HEFCE research funding policy, *Higher Education Funding Council for England* (2)

Higher Education Quality Council (HEQC) Academic Quality Assurance Group (1997) *Academic Quality Audit: The University of Exeter*, HEQC, London [Online] http://www.qaa.ac.uk/revreps/instrev/exeter/foreword.htm

Hoagland (2001) Personal communication

Huber, M T (2000) Disciplinary styles in the scholarship of teaching: reflections on the Carnegie Academy for the Scholarship of Teaching and Learning, in *Improving Student Learning Through the Disciplines*, ed C Rust, pp 20–31, Oxford Centre for Staff and Learning Development, Oxford

Huber, M T (2001) Designing careers around the scholarship of teaching, *Change*, **33** (4), pp 21–29

Huber, M and Morreale, S (2002) *Disciplinarity in the Scholarship of Teaching and Learning: Exploring common ground*, American Association for Higher Education and the Foundation for the Advancement of Learning, Washington, DC

Hughes, C, and Tight, M (1995) Linking university teaching and research, *Higher Education Review*, **28** (1), pp 51–65

Hughes, P, Blair, D, Clear-Hill, H and Halewood, C (2001) Local sustainability and LA21: a vertically integrated research, learning and teaching activity, *Planet*, (2) pp 5–7

Hutchings, P and Shulman, L S (1999) The scholarship of teaching: new elaborations, new developments, *Change*, **31** (5), pp 11–15

ILT News (2002) New Individual Entry Route [On line] http://www.ilt.ac.uk/news/n20020708.html

Jenkins, A (1995a) The impact of the Research Assessment Exercises on teaching in selected geography departments in England and Wales, *Geography*, **84** (4), pp 367–74

Jenkins, A (1995b) The Research Assessment Exercise, funding and teaching quality, *Quality Assurance in Education*, **3** (2), pp 4–12

Jenkins, A (1998) Assessing David Blunkett on teaching and research, *Teaching Forum*, Oxford Brookes University, **45** (Spring), p 8

Jenkins, A (2000a) Where does geography stand on the relationship between teaching and research. Where do we stand and deliver? *Journal of Geography in Higher Education*, **24** (3), pp 325–51

Jenkins, A (2000b) Rs and gripes? Head for the US, *Times Higher Education Supplement* (June), p 44

Jenkins, A J, Blackman, T, Lindsay, R O and Paton-Saltzberg, R (1998) Teaching and research: student perceptions and policy implications, *Studies in Higher Education*, **23** (2), pp 127–41

Jensen, J-J (1988) Research and teaching in the universities of Denmark: does such an interplay really exist? *Higher Education*, **17**, pp 17–26

JM Consulting (2000) *Interactions between Research, Teaching, and Other Academic Activities: Report for HEFCE*, Higher Education Consulting Group, Bristol

Johnston, C (2000) *Fostering Deeper Learning*, University of Melbourne, Victoria

Johnston, R J (1998) Dearing and research, *Journal of Geography in Higher Education*, **22** (1), pp 72–81

Jungck, J (1997) Realities of radical reform: reconstructing 'chilly climates' into 'collaborative communities' – sharing BioQUEST experience, in *Student-Active Science: Models for innovation in college science teaching*, ed A McNeal and C D'Avanzo, Saunders College Publishing, London

Kemmis, S, Marginson, S, Porter, P and Rizvi, F (1999) *Enhancing Diversity in Australian Higher Education*, University of Western Australia, Australia

Krahenbuhl, G S (1998) Faculty work, *Change*, November–December, pp 19–25

Kreber, C and Cranton, P (2000) Fragmentation versus integration of faculty work, in *To Improve the Academy: Resources for faculty, instructional, and organisational development*, no 18, ed M Kaplan, POD Network, Bolton

Krochalk, P C and Hope, E (1995) A framework for integrating faculty discipline-related research with classroom teaching and learning, *Journal on Excellence in College Teaching*, **6** (2), pp 3–15

Kuh, G D and Hu, S (2001) Learning productivity at research universities, *Journal of Higher Education*, **72** (1), pp 1–28

Kyvik, S and Smeby, J-C (1994) Teaching and research: the relationship between the supervision of graduate students and faculty research performance, *Higher Education*, **28**, pp 227–39

Latham, J (2001) Personal communication

Leary, M R and Williams, J E (1988) A system for balancing departmental teaching and research, *Journal of Social Behaviour and Personality*, **3** (2), pp 119–23

Legge, K (1997) *Problem-Orientated Group Project Work at Roskilde University*, Roskilde University, Roskilde

Lindsay, R (1998) Teaching and research: the missing link, *Teaching Forum*, Oxford Brookes University, **45** (Spring), pp 9–11

Lindsay, R and Paton-Saltzberg, R (1993) *The Effects of Paid Employment on the Academic Performance of Full-Time Students in a British 'New' University: Report for the Academic Standards Committee of Oxford Brookes University*, Oxford Brookes University, Oxford

Lindsay, R, Breen, R and Jenkins, A (2002) Academic research and teaching quality: the views of undergraduate and postgraduate students, *Studies in Higher Education*, **27** (3), pp 309–27

Macquarie University (2000) *Macquarie University Strategic Directions 2000*, Macquarie University, Sydney, Australia

Marginson, S (2000) Rethinking academic work in the global era, *Journal of Higher Education Policy and Management*, **22** (1), pp 25–35

Marincovitch, M and Reis, R (2000) *An Invitation to C R E A T E : Creating Research Example Across the Teaching Enterprise – American Association for Higher Education: Forum on Faculty Roles and Rewards*, American Association for Higher Education, New Orleans, La.

Marsh, H and Hattie, J (forthcoming) The relation between research productivity and teaching effectiveness: complementary, antagonistic, or independent constructs? *Journal of Higher Education*

Marsh, H W and Roche, L A (1997) Making students' evaluations of teaching effectiveness effective, *American Psychologist*, **52** (11), pp 1187–97

Martin, E, Benjamin, J, Prosser, M and Trigwell, K (1999) Scholarship of teaching: a study of the approaches of academic staff, in Proceedings of the 1998 6th International Symposium Improving Student Learning: Improving Student Learning Outcomes, ed C Rust, pp 326–31, Oxford Centre for Staff and Learning Development, Oxford Brookes University [Online] http://www.epig.rmit.edu.au/dst/Paper_1. stm

Marton, F and Saljo, R (1976) On qualitative differences in learning: outcomes and process, *British Journal of Educational Psychology*, **46**, pp 4–11

Maslow, A H (1970) *Motivation and Personality*, 2nd edn, Harper, New York

McCartney, S, and Brown, R B (1995) Research learning on the Essex MBA, in *Research Teaching and Learning in Higher Education*, ed B Smith and S Brown, pp 153–64, Kogan Page, London

McClelland, D C, Atkinson, J W, Clark, R A and Clark, E L (1953) *The Achievement Motive*, Appleton-Century-Crofts, New York

McCormick, A C (2000a) Bringing the Carnegie Classification into the 21st century, *American Association for Higher Education Bulletin*, **52** (5), pp 3–15

McCormick, A C (2000b) *The Carnegie Classification of Institutes of Higher Education*, Carnegie Association, Stanford [Online] http:Carnegiefoundation/org/Classification/CIHE2000/background.htm

McNay, I (1997a) *The Impact of the 1992 RAE on Institutional and Individual behaviour in English Higher Education: The evidence from a research project*, Higher Education Funding Council for England (HEFCE), Bristol

McNay, I (1997b) *The Impact of the 1992 Research Assessment on Institutional and Individual Behaviour in English Higher Education: Summary report and commentary*, Anglia Polytechnic University, Chelmsford

McNay, I (1998) The paradoxes of research assessment and funding, in *Changing Relationships between Higher Education and the State*, ed M Henkel and B Little, pp 191–203, Jessica Kingsley, London

McNeal, A P (2000) Personal communication

McNeal, A P and D'Avanzo, C (1997) *Student Active Science: Models of innovation in college science teaching*, Saunders College Publishing, Fort Worth, Texas

McQueen, K G, Taylor, G, Brown, M C and Mayer, W (1990) Integration of teaching and research in a regional geological mapping project, *Journal of Geological Education*, **38**, pp 88–93

Meade, P and Woodhouse, D (2000) Evaluating the effectiveness of the New Zealand Academic Audit Unit: review and outcomes, *Quality in Higher Education*, **6** (1), pp 19–29

Moses, I (1990) Teaching, research and scholarship in different disciplines, *Higher Education*, **19**, pp 351–375

Murray, R E G (2001) Integrating teaching and research through writing development for students and staff, *Active Learning in Higher Education*, **2** (1), pp 31–45

National Committee of Enquiry into Higher Education (NCIHE) (1963) *Committee on Higher Education* (the Robbins Report), HMSO, London (Cmnd 2154)

NCIHE (1997) *Higher Education in the Learning Society: Report of the National Committee of Enquiry into Higher Education* (the Dearing Report), HMSO, London

National Science Foundation (NSF) (1995) *NSF in a Changing World: the National Science Foundation's strategic plan*, National Science Foundation, Washington, DC

NSF (1997) *Recognition Rewards for the Integration of Research and Education (RAIRE)*, National Science Foundation, Washington, DC

NSF (1998) *Research Experiences for Undergraduates: Program announcement*, National Science Foundation, Washington, DC

Nelson, M (2000) *Undergraduate Research: An educational force in the new millennium*, American Associates for Higher Education: Forum on faculty roles and rewards, New Orleans, La.

Neumann, R (1993a) Research and scholarship: perceptions of senior academic administrators, *Higher Education*, **25**, pp 97–110

Neumann, R (1993b) academic work: perceptions of senior academic administrators, *Australian Educational Researcher*, **20** (1), pp 33–47

Neumann, R (1994) The teaching–research nexus: applying a framework to university students' learning experiences, *European Journal of Education*, **29** (3), pp 323–39

Neumann, R and Guthrie, J (2001) The Corporisation of Research in Higher Education, *Macquarie Working Papers in Management*, Sydney, Macquarie University

Neumann, R, Parry, S and Becher, T (2002) Teaching and learning in their disciplinary contexts: a conceptual analysis, *Studies in Higher Education*,

Newby, H (1999) Higher education in the 21st century: some possible futures, *Perspectives*, **3** (4), pp 106–13

Newby, H (2001) Opinion: excellence should be rewarded in areas other than research, or else we risk losing quality, *Guardian Education*, November 13, p 15

Newby, H (2002) Opinion: sometimes it is useful to stand and stare as long as we remember we will be judged on our practice, *Guardian Education*, February 13, p 13

Nicholls, G (2001) *Professional Development in Higher Education*, London, Kogan Page

Nixon, J (1997) Regenerating professionalism within the academic workplace, in *The End of Professions? The restructuring of professional work*, ed J Broadbent, M Dietrch and J Roberts, Routledge, London, pp 86–103

Novotny, H et al (2000) *Rethinking Science: Knowledge and the public in an age of uncertainty*, Polity, Cambridge

Oehme, F and Seitzer, D (2000) Learn by doing: how to include new requirements of research in engineering education, *European Journal of Engineering Education*, **25** (2), pp 131–37

Office of the Associate Minister for Education (2002) *Tertiary Education Strategy*, Wellington, New Zealand

Olesen, H S and Jensen, J H (1999) Can 'the university' be revived in 'late modernity'? in *Project Studies: A late modern university reform?* ed H S Olesen and J H Jensen, Roskilde University Press

Ontario Council on University Affairs (1994) *Undergraduate Teaching, Research and Consulting/Community Service: What are the functional interactions?* Ontario Council on University Affairs, Toronto, Canada

Paewai, S and Suddaby, G (eds) (2001) *Towards Understanding the Interdependence of Research and Teaching: Occasional papers from the Vice Chancellor's Symposium on the Research Teaching Nexus*, Massey University, Palmerston North

Paewai, S and Suddaby, G (2002) Personal communication

Paget, E, Mainprize, B, James, T and Watt, J (2001) personal communication

Pajares, F (1996) Motivation in academic settings, *Review of Educational Research*, **66** (4), pp 543–78

Parlett, M (1977) The department as a learning milieu, *Studies in Higher Education*, **2**, pp 171–81

Parlett, M R and King, J G (1971) *Concentrated Study: A pedagogic innovation observed*, Society for Research in Higher Education, London

Pascarella, E T and Terenzini, P T (1991) *How College Affects Students*, Jossey-Bass, San Francisco, Calif.

Patrick, W J and Stanley, E C (1998) Teaching and Research Quality Indicators and the shaping of higher education, *Research in Higher Education*, **39** (1), pp 19–41

Perkins, J (1998) Integrating research and teaching, *Teaching Forum*, 45 (Spring), pp 3–4

Perkins, J (2002) Linking research and teaching and re-designing the undergraduate modular programme, *Teaching News*, Oxford Brookes University, February, pp 1–2 [Online] http://www.brookes.ac.uk/virtual/NewTF/tn/ tnfeb2002.html

Perry, W (1970) *Forms of Intellectual and Ethical Development in the College Years: A scheme*, Holt, Rinehart and Winston, Troy, Mich.

Piper, M (2001) Presidential Address, University of British Colombia [Online] www.vision.ubc.ca/supp_docs/piper_bog.html

Poinsot, D (2001) Personal communication

Pope, R (1998) Pope takes line on research and teaching, *Teaching Forum*, **45** (Spring), pp 5–7

Prince, G S and Kelly, N (1997) Hampshire College as a model for progressive science education, in *Student Active Science: Models of innovation in college science teaching*, ed A P McNeal and C D'Avanzo, Saunders College Publishing, Fort Worth, Texas

Quality Assurance Agency (QAA) (2000) *Benchmark Statement for English*, Quality Assurance Agency, Gloucester

QAA (2001) *The Framework for Higher Education Qualifications in England, Wales and Northern Ireland*, Quality Assurance Agency, Gloucester [Online] www.qaa.ac.uk

Rameley, J A (1997) Creating a supportive environment for major curricula changes, in *Student Active Science: Models of innovation in college science teaching*, ed A P McNeal and C D'Avanzo, Saunders College Publishing, Fort Worth, Texas

Ramsden, P (1998) *Influences on Academic Work: Learning to lead in higher education*, Routledge, London

Ramsden, P (2001) Strategic management of teaching and learning, in *Improving Student Learning Strategically*, ed C Rust, pp 1–10, OCSLD, Oxford

Ramsden, P, and Moses, I (1992) Associations between research and teaching in Australian Higher Education, *Higher Education*, **23** (3), pp 273–95

Ramsden, P, Margetson, D, Martin, E and Clarke, S (1998) *Recognising and Rewarding Good Teaching in Higher Education in Australian Higher Education*, Committee for the Advancement of University Teaching, Canberra

Reid, I (2001) What is needed to make Australia a knowledge-driven and learning-driven society? *Business/Higher Education Round Table*, Melbourne

Rice, E R (1992) Toward a broader conception of scholarship: the American context, in *Research and Higher Education: The United Kingdom and the United States*, ed T G Whiston and R Geiger, pp 117–29, Open University and Society for Research in Higher Education Press, Buckingham

Roach, M, Blackmore, P and Dempster, J (2001) Supporting high-level learning through research-based methods: a framework for course development, *Innovations in Education and Teaching International*, **38** (4), pp 369–82

Robertson, J (1999) What do academics value? Experiences of the relation between teaching and research, Paper presented at the HERDSA conference, Melbourne

Robertson, J and Bond, C (2001) Experiences of the relation between teaching and research: what do academics value? *Higher Education Research and Development*, **20** (1), pp 5–19

Rogers, J (1999) Research Assessment 2001: research into teaching, *Teaching in Higher Education*, **4** (2), pp 285–86

Rosengarten, H (2000) Personal communication

Rotter, J B (1982) Social learning theory, in *Expectations and Actions: Expectancy-value models in psychology*, ed N T Feather, pp 241–60, Lawrence Erlbaum, Hillsdale, NJ

Rowland, S (1996) Relationships between teaching and research, *Teaching in Higher Education*, **1** (1), pp 7–20

Rowland, S (2000) *The Enquiring University Teacher*, Open University Press, Buckingham

Rust, C (2000) *Improving Student Learning Through the Disciplines*, Oxford Centre for Staff and Learning Development, Oxford

Ryder, J and Leach, J (1997) Research projects in the undergraduate science course: students learning about science through enculturation, in *Improving Student Learning: Improving Student Learning Through Course Design*, ed C Rust and G Gibbs, pp 246–53, Oxford Centre for Staff and Learning Development, Oxford

Savin-Baden, M (2000) *Problem-Based Learning in Higher Education: Untold stories*, Society for Research in Higher Education and Open University Press, Buckingham

Schimank, U and Winnes, M (2000) Beyond Humbolt? The relationship between teaching and research in European university systems, *Science and Public Policy*, **27** (6), pp 397–408

Scobey, D (2002) Putting the academy in its place, *Places*, forthcoming

Searleman, A, and Herrmann, D (1994) *Memory from a Broader Perspective*, McGraw-Hill, London

Seitzer, D (2000) Research and engineering education, *European Journal of Engineering Education*, **25** (2), pp 111–13

Seligman, M E P (1975) *On Depression, Development and Death*, Freeman, San Francisco, Calif.

Seltzer, T, and Bentley, K S (1999) *The Creative Age: Knowledge and skills for the new economy*, Demos, London

Shulman, L S (2000) Foreword to the *Carnegie Classification of Institutions of Higher Education*, Carnegie Foundation, Stanford [Online] http://www.carnegiefoundation.org/whatsnew/index.htm

Sidaway, J D (1997) The production of British geography, *Transactions of the Institute of British Geographers*, **22**, pp 488–504

Smeby, J-C (1998) Knowledge production and knowledge transmission: the interaction between research and teaching at universities, *Teaching in Higher Education*, **3** (1), pp 7–20

Smeby, J-C (2002) Consequences of project organisation in graduate education, *Studies in Higher Education*, **7** (2), pp 139–51

Snyder, B R (1971) *The Hidden Curriculum*, Knopf, New York

Southampton Institute (1998) *Research and Scholarship at Southampton Institute Conference*, Southampton Institute, Southampton

Southampton Institute (2000) *Draft Document Identifying Action to Implement the Strategies for Learning, Teaching and Curriculum Development, and for Research and Scholarship*, Southampton Institute, Southampton

Spronken-Smith, R, Jennings, J, Robertson, J, Mein-Smith, P, Vincent, G and Wake, G (2000) *The Research Teaching Link at Canterbury*, University of Canterbury, Christchurch, New Zealand

Staff and Educational Development Association (SEDA) (2000) *Submission to the Fundamental Review of Research*, Staff and Educational Development Association, Birmingham

Stanier, L (1995) Student projects in collaboration with a Family Health Services authority, *Journal of Geography in Higher Education*, **19** (2), pp 203–06

Stark, J S and Lattuca, L R (1997) *Shaping the College Curriculum: Academic plans in action*, Allyn and Bacon, Needham Heights, Mass.

Strike, K A and Posner, G J (1985) A conceptual change view of learning and understanding, in *Cognitive Structure and Conceptual Change,* ed L West and L Pines, pp 147–76, Academic Press, New York

Strike, K A and Posner, G J (1992) A revisionist theory of conceptual change, in *Philosophy of Science, Cognitive Psychology, and Educational Theory and Practice*, ed R Duschl and R Hamilton, pp 147–76, SUNY, New York

Suddaby, G (2000) *The Vice Chancellor's Symposium on the Research–Teaching Nexus*, Massey University, Palmerston

Suddaby, G (2001) Auditing the teaching/research nexus at Massey University, Public lecture, Oxford Brookes University, March 22 [Online] http://www.brookes.ac.uk/schools/planning/LTRC/Links/Teaching-Research%20Nexus/index.htm

Suddaby, G and St George, A (2002) *The Nature of Tertiary Teaching*, Massey University, Palmerston North, New Zealand

Sundberg, M (1997) Assessing the effectiveness of an investigative laboratory to confront common misconceptions in life sciences, in *Student-Active Science: Models of innovation in college science teaching,* ed A McNeal and C D'Avanzo, Saunders College Publishing, London

Terenzini, P T and Pascarella, E T (1994) Living with myths: undergraduate education in America, *Change*, January/February, pp 28–32

Tertiary Education Advisory Commission (2001) *Shaping the Funding Framework*, Tertiary Education Advisory Commission, Wellington, New Zealand

Thompson, J B (1988) The use of intensive workshops in the teaching of computer studies students, *Journal of Education and Computing*, **4**, pp 59–69

Tulving, E (1985) How many memory systems are there? *American Psychologist*, **40**, pp 385–98

UK Central Council for Nursing, Midwifery and Health Visiting (2000) *Requirements for Pre-registration and Nursing Programmes*, UK Central Council for Nursing, Midwives and Health Visiting

University of Auckland (2000) *Academic Audit Portfolio*, University of Auckland, New Zealand

University of Birmingham (2000) *Learning and Teaching Strategy*, University of Birmingham

University of British Columbia (2000a) *Trek 2000: A vision for the 21st century*, University of British Columbia, Vancouver, Canada [Online] www.vision.ubc.ca/supp_docs/piper_bog.html

University of British Columbia (2000b) *University of British Columbia Academic Plan*, University of British Columbia, Vancouver, Canada

University of Canterbury (2000) *Audit 2000: A portfolio presented to the Audit Panel*, University of Canterbury, Christchurch, New Zealand

University of Stony Brook (1998) The Boyer Commission, *Reinventing Undergraduate Education: A blueprint for America's research universities*, Stony Brook, New York

University of Waikato (1999) *Strategic Plan for Research and Postgraduate Studies*, University of Waikato, Waikato, New Zealand

University of Western Australia (2001) *Guidelines for the Establishment and Review of UWA Centres*, University of Western Australia, Perth, Australia

Volkwein, J F and Carbone, D A (1994) The impact of departmental research and teaching climates on undergraduate growth and satisfaction, *Journal of Higher Education*, **65** (2), pp 147–67

Weaver, F S (1989) *Promoting Inquiry in Undergraduate Learning* (pp 1–15), Jossey-Bass, London

Webster, F (2001) Personal communication

Willis, D (2001) Building local partnerships between teaching and research: the impact of national policy and audit, Annual Conference of the Higher Education Research and Development Society of Australasia, University of Newcastle, Australia

Wills, J (1996) Labouring for love? A comment on academics and their hours of work, *Antipode*, **38** (3), pp 292–303

Wilson, R (2002) Boyer Commission says colleges have been making improvements sought in 1998 report, *Chronicle of Higher Education*, March 8

Winn, S (1995) Learning by doing: teaching research methods through student participation in a commissioned research project, *Studies in Higher Education*, **20** (2), pp 203–14

Winn, S (2001) Personal communication

Woodhouse, D (1998) Auditing research and the research/teaching nexus, *New Zealand Journal of Educational Studies*, **33** (1), pp 39–53

Woodhouse, D (2001) The teaching/research nexus: lessons from New Zealand audits, presentation at the VC Symposium: The Teaching–Research Nexus:

Enhancing the Links, University of Wollongong, 3 October [Online] http://cedir.uow.edu.au/nexus/dwoodhse.html

Wright, A and O'Neil, C (1995) Teaching improvement practices: international perspectives, in *Teaching Improvement Practices*, ed A Wright, pp 1–57, Anker, Bolton, Mass.

Wright, P and Williams, P (2001) How it all fits together: Quality Assurance and the standards infrastructure, *Higher Quality*, **9** (November), pp 11–12

Yorke, M (2000) A cloistered virtue? Pedagogical research and policy in UK higher education, *Higher Education Quarterly*, **54** (2), pp 106–26

Zamorski, B (2000) *Research-Led Teaching and Learning in Higher Education*, Centre for Applied Research in Education, Norwich

Zetter, R (2002) From Perkins to Jenkins: filling the implementation gap, *Teaching News*, Oxford Brookes University, February, pp 5–7 [Online] http://www.brookes.ac.uk/virtual/NewTF/tn/tnfeb2002.html

Zinn, M B and Eitzen, D S (2000) Nurturing graduate students: integrative scholarship through textbook projects, *Teaching Sociology*, **28**, pp 364–69

Zubrick, A, Reid, I and Rossiter, P (2001) *Strengthening the Nexus between Teaching and Research*, Australian Department of Education, Training and Youth Affairs, Canberra

Further reading

Astin, A W (1996) Involvement in learning revisited: lessons we have learned, *Journal of College Student Development*, **37** (2), pp 123–34

Baxter Magolda, M B, Boes, L, Hollis, M L and Jaramillo, D L (1998) *Impact of the Undergraduate Summer Scholar Experience on Epistemological Development*, University of Miami, Fla.

Biggs, J (1979) Individual differences in study processes and the quality of learning outcomes, *Higher Education*, **8**, pp 381–94

Biggs, J (1999) *Teaching for Quality Learning at University: What the student does*, Society for Research in Higher Education and Open University Press, Buckingham

Breen, R, and Lindsay, R (2002) Different disciplines require different motivation for student success, *Research in Higher Education*, **43** (3)

Elton, L (1999) *Research and Teaching: Are there casual relationships?* Higher Education Research and Development Unit, University College London

Elton, L (1999) *Research and Teaching: What are the real relationships?* Higher Universities Research and Development Unit, University College London

Gibbs, G (1995) Research into student learning, in *Research, Teaching and Learning in Higher Education*, ed B Smith and S Brown, Kogan Page, London

Jenkins, A (1988) Teaching and research revisited, *Area*, **20**, pp 151–64

Jenkins, A (2000) *The Relationship Between Research and Teaching in Higher Education: Present realities, future possibilities*, Southampton Institute and the Higher Education Funding Council for England

Jenkins, A (2000) Review of the research and scholarly evidence on teaching/research relationships in higher education, paper presented at the Seminar on Teaching/Research Relationships, Southampton Institute

Jenkins, A (2000) Steering the RAE juggernaut: have we missed the boat? *Educational Developments*, (November), pp 1–4

New Zealand Universities Academic Audit Unit (2000) *The University of Auckland: Academic Audit Report*, New Zealand Universities Academic Audit Unit, Wellington, NZ

Ramsden, P (1998) Managing the effective university, *Higher Education Research and Development*, **17** (3), pp 347–71

Savin-Baden, M and Wilkie, K (2000) Understanding and utilising problem-based learning strategically in higher education, in C Rust (ed) *Improving Student Learning Strategically*, Oxford Centre for Staff Development, Oxford, pp 151–60

University of Canterbury (2000) *The Research–Teaching Link at Canterbury: A report prepared for the Teaching and Learning Committee by a joint sub-committee comprising members of the Teaching and Learning Committee and the Research Committee*, University of Canterbury, Christchurch, New Zealand

University of Southampton (2000) *Learning and Teaching Strategy* [Online] www.clt.soton.ac.uk/lts

Willis, D, Harper, J and Sawicka, T (1999) Putting the worms back in the can: encouraging diversity in the teaching research nexus, paper presented at the HERDSA Conference, Melbourne

Index